LOVE
IS THE
REASON

CHRISTIAN COMPASSION
AND THE CHALLENGE OF SECULARISM

BY DAVID C POTTER MBE

To the memory of
Rachel

whose life has enriched the lives of thousands
of people with learning disabilities, their families
and their friends, and her own family above all.

1963 - 2012

CONTENTS

APPENDICES

ACKNOWLEDGEMENTS   P 116

Scripture quotations are from the New International Version (NIV) of the Bible, 1995 edition.

PREFACE

Nola Leach, Chief Executive, CARE

'Go into the world uncorrupted, a breath of fresh air in this polluted society. Provide people with a glimpse of good living and the living God.'

I love this Message version of Paul's words to the Philippian Christians. (Philippians 2:14) It is as relevant for Christians today as they were when he wrote them two thousand years ago. There are those today who are committed to an agenda to minimise, if not totally remove, any Christian influence from our nation's life. We face increasing challenges, and yet there are huge opportunities for God's people to bring that 'breath of fresh air' into every sector of society. The Christian message of hope and justice is needed more than ever in the twenty-first century.

For us in CARE, just as in Prospects, the human dignity of each man and woman, girl and boy, made in the image of God, is the golden thread running through all we do. CARE's mandate of bringing Christian truth to bear on the nation's life is one side of our work along with doing all we can to demonstrate God's love in action - a powerful motivating force.

In this book David refreshingly and skilfully examines and illustrates the difference between Christian motivation and that of others who provide care. Of course, much great work is done by both people of faith and those who have none. Christian involvement, however, brings in an extra dimension because our motivating force is obedience to our loving God. Being called to speak out and care for the vulnerable affects our values, freedoms and sense of justice. This is what drives God's people in a broken world.

Sometimes Christians can become disheartened and think that there is no longer a space for them in the public square. But there is! This book powerfully argues the case that we have a high privilege and every right to be there.

We believe that Jesus is Lord. Abraham Kuyper, the Dutch theologian and Prime Minister of the Netherlands between 1901 and 1905 wrote these inspiring words: 'In the total expanse of human life there is not a single square inch of which Christ, who alone is sovereign, does not declare "That is mine!"'

From the early commission in Genesis to 'fill the earth and subdue it' through the prophet Jeremiah's call to 'work for the good of the city' and to uphold justice for the vulnerable, up to Jesus' example of loving others, the Bible's message is clear. We are called to serve and to care. This is the outworking of our salvation.

This book clearly shows that we as Christians have a better way of working, simply because we are motivated by the love of Christ. It will empower those who may feel that opportunities to show God's love in action are being taken from them. The evidence on the ground attests to the breadth and quality of Christian caring, work that, because of its effectiveness, is being sought by many in authority. Prospects is an outstanding example of this.

CARE has been privileged over the years to partner with Prospects on various occasions. Both Lyndon Bowring, CARE's Executive Chairman and I are thrilled to be Ambassadors for them and commend this book very warmly.

PREFACE

Jonathan Edwards, Executive Ambassador of Prospects

Christians are not merely a minority in our society but a small minority. That stark fact confronts the church with enormous challenges. It would be wise for the Christian community to assume that society will seek to squeeze and marginalise it even more in the years to come. The church, therefore, needs desperately to reflect on its place in society and to discover afresh its calling to be a distinctive Christ-shaped community.

David Potter addresses these crucial issues out of his passionate commitment to working with people with learning disabilities. His long experience gives him every right to speak and his honest wrestling with the issues will come as an encouragement and challenge to everyone who wants to follow Christ wholeheartedly in this secular age.

David's roots are not so very different from my own. Conservative evangelicalism used to struggle with any engagement with society out of a fear that it would distract from the proclamation of the Gospel. The social gospel was considered to be the preserve of those who had lost confidence in the liberating gospel of Jesus Christ. But David and I have travelled since those days. Like most evangelicals we would want to affirm the crucial importance of loving people in their entirety and not just one aspect of their lives. Jesus wants everyone to know his love and forgiveness, but he also wants to reach out to their physical, financial and social needs.

Prospects, the charity which David and his wife founded, is a dynamic demonstration of Christian love to people with learning disabilities. The growth of the organization is heart warming. Thousands of people with learning disabilities and their families have been touched by the ministry of Prospects. But there is no space for complacency. Prospects is being squeezed by the demands of an increasingly secular and, at times, anti-Christian society. This demands that Prospects continues to reflect on its place in society, and the way in which it does its work.

Most of the people who work for Prospects are practising Christians. The organization has always been at pains to point out that it recognises that Christians do not have a monopoly on compassion and care. That would be offensive nonsense. Many non-Christian people pour out their lives in loving and sacrificial service to others, and that should be celebrated. But the motivation behind Prospects is the love of Christ himself, and the ministry that is exercised is intended to be one that reflects Christ and commends his love to others.

Prospects is, therefore, dependent on large numbers of Christian people being willing to give support to people with learning disabilities. That has always proved difficult and is acutely challenging at the moment. This very practical need for staff sharply focuses the issues which David raises in this book. Are we really willing to turn our compassionate Christian convictions into action? Are we committed to ensuring that our churches are not merely places to celebrate the grace and mercy of God, but living communities of love, sacrifice and compassion? And most sharply of all - are we, individually, willing to make the sacrifice ourselves?

FOREWORD

David Potter, Prospects, 2013

The three of us, Mum, my brother and me, huddled round the feeble fire in our over-furnished 'front room' - the working class equivalent of a lounge or drawing room. My baby brother was asleep upstairs but our hushed tones were not for fear of waking him. We knew we must not disturb Dad's meeting. 'Dad's meeting' seemed to happen often but was probably only monthly. A group of four or five men would take over our basement living room, where the fire was kept burning and the room was warm, for the regular committee meeting of the Reading branch of the Communist Party. Dad was the Secretary and acknowledged leader of this group. They were not the revolutionaries of popular imagination but genuinely compassionate men whose main preoccupation, it seemed to me, was for poor people living on a large council estate south of the town. The Party saw it as their mission to campaign for lower rents and better conditions for the residents of the estate. The fact that most of the people took what concessions they gained with little appreciation seemed not to dim the Party's commitment to the cause.

Those meetings were shaping my own outlook more than I realised. When I later began to attend Boys' Brigade at the Baptist church round the corner from home, I was surprised to find that they had little interest in the impoverished people living in the hovels behind the church building. In fact they were at pains to show that there was no hint of a 'social gospel' in their ministry. Evangelism took them on marches of witness round the narrow streets with a Gospel sermon at strategic points, but nothing more practical was done to ease the very real poverty and need which lay in the cramped housing between the church and the town centre.

After I became a Christian and began to read the Bible myself, I was struck by the discovery that it has a great deal to say about people who are poor, or in need. God seemed far more concerned for them than was evident in the Christians I knew at that time. While it was clear that there was no way one could earn salvation by 'do gooding', it was equally clear that love for one's neighbour was mandatory. As the years passed I felt that there must be more balance in my own life and, in due course, ministry.

Another living room, this time a summer night, a young woman struggled to give birth, attended by doctor and midwife and watched by her anxious young husband. The struggle had already lasted for hours and would last a good few more but, with the help of caring professionals, Madeleine was finally delivered of a baby daughter who was then wrapped in a towel and thrust into my waiting arms, for I was the anxious husband. As any parent knows, it is an experience like no other. To say that it is life-changing is vastly to understate its impact. But in our case it was to do so to a degree we could not know or imagine on 13 August 1961 and, in doing so, it would form a bridge with that other night in that other living room. On that same day I received a call to become pastor of Little Ilford Baptist Church in East Ham, London. That, we believed, set my 'career' on its course.

We were to learn some six weeks after the birth that our baby Rachel had what we now call Down's syndrome. In the years that followed we were to meet more and more families whose lives were locked into the needs and concerns that a person with a learning disability brings with them. As the incidence of learning disability is more common in babies born to older couples, we found that the most common concern voiced by them was simply this: 'Who will care when we can no longer do so?' Perhaps it is not surprising that, with the sort of background we had, Madeleine and I began to campaign for a Christian response to the issue. And it is probably also unsurprising that the general reaction was, 'Well, do something!' So we founded A Cause for Concern, now known as Prospects. (See Appendix E)

That was in 1976 and, in the ensuing years, as Prospects has grown into the substantial organisation it has become, I have read and studied the Bible, numerous books and articles, and have attended seminars, lectures, sermons and studies in an attempt to understand more fully God's heart for people who are needy or disadvantaged. How should we respond? What should we do? Where do we find the resources of love, energy and money for any action we take? Is this a job for the Church, the local church, or just the individual - or should it be left to professionals and the State?

This study is the fruit of years of reflection around these themes. It was initiated by a request from Prospects and CARE Trust to write a Christian response to such questions for people who are 'hands on' in the many Christian charities and agencies working with and for the people in our communities, and for those campaigners who speak up for people who are voiceless in the places where policies are made and laws passed. It is intended to support and assist those who today stand where the action is and give practical expression to the powerful mandate of God's Word. To succeed in being relevant it must be relevant in the now substantially secular society in which we live, where humanist attitudes and ideals are increasingly to the fore.

If you are going to journey comfortably with me through this study you need to know my direction of travel and my intended destination. My aim is to address two questions (and perhaps find some answers!). The first is almost as old as humanity itself and has preoccupied thinking men and women for at least as long as there has been writing: 'What is man?' - by which is meant human beings and not just males, of course[1]. What is it about human beings that makes us feel we are distinctive? The second question is related to the first and is, perhaps, more modern: 'Why should we care?' - about other people, that is. We suspect that people used to be more caring than they are nowadays, more supportive in their extended, less mobile families and in their pre-industrial communities. Our lives are more atomised today with the State expected to look after us - isn't that what we pay our taxes for? But the structures of the welfare society are crumbling under the strain of increased demand and spiralling cost, so who will ensure that vulnerable and needy people are cared about and cared for in the future?

Christians are as much affected by these questions as are other members of society and we need to ask whether there is a distinctively Christian answer to both the questions posed. And in looking for answers I hope to provide a Biblical rationale for the work in which countless Christians are already engaged. My starting point is the Bible because I take it to be the Word of God. It does not pose our questions directly, but we will find no better place to look for the answers. My hope is that we will better understand God's mind and heart for people, especially those who are vulnerable. I hope too that it will give you greater confidence in what you believe so that you are better able to face the challenges of the future, for it seems probable that the world around us will demand an explanation of us for our faith. You may not always agree with what I write, but it may provide raw material to help you think Biblically and to find your own answers.

---

[1]   The use of 'man' to refer to all humans has been retained only where it is used in a quotation.

CHAPTER ONE
THE WORLD ABOUT US

A CRISIS OF CARING?

There is a problem in Britain today: the difficulty is working out just what it is! The topic that has been at or near the top of every news bulletin for the last few years at least is the economy - or The Economy. The euro, interest rates, unemployment, bank bonuses, austerity, redundancy, cuts, taxation - there is a whole vocabulary of terms which were once the province of economists and are now part of our common tongue. I have lived long enough to know that when the country faces economic difficulties on the current scale then measures are taken to cut government spending. Services are cut, efficiencies are 'found', redundancies are required, wages are frozen. Reaction takes the form of strikes, marches, protests, pickets and noisy council meetings. Those who cost governments most in benefits and pensions and services - those who are most vulnerable and voiceless - are likely to be further disadvantaged. The economics are simple: care costs!

But is it only an economic problem? Do you remember the year there were repeated reports of stabbings and shootings on English streets. Hardly a day seemed to pass without another incident on the national news: a row had broken out in an Oxford Street shoe store between young customers, and suddenly a teenager lay dead on the pavement among the throng of Christmas shoppers. Then there was the student going to buy a Big Mac who was stopped and shot in the head at close range by a complete stranger. Soon such stories were relegated to local news to give place to whole families found dead in their home. A father had 'lost it' and shot his wife and children before turning the gun on himself. Then a mother ran screaming from her blazing house while three of her children were trapped inside; suspected arson. On and on

We watched the end of year reviews on TV and saw again the mindless August riots and the rampaging groups of people ransacking shops, throwing bricks and flaming torches at police, burning down shops and houses. The police were stunned at being upstaged by the speed at which the rioters moved from place to place and the riots from city to city. The Government condemned, the bishops intoned and the tabloid headline writers had a field day. These things happened in the run up to Christmas 2011, but it could have been one of several periods in recent years.

At a similar time there were reports on the standard of care given to elderly people in hospitals and nursing homes. Could it really be true that old people became more ill by going to hospital where they had hoped to be made well again? But we read of them being malnourished for want of help and care.

A report about attacks on people with learning disabilities made shocking reading as more than half of them reported abuse and discrimination. An inquiry into disability-related harassment reported 'an awful lot of unpleasant things happening to a great many people, almost certainly in the hundreds of thousands each year.'[1] The report gives ten case-studies of the terrible suffering endured by people with disabilities at the hands of other people.

Now it may be that these things happen frequently and it was coincidence that brought them together and focussed my attention. I'm not sure this is so, but still they raise a serious question: does anybody care? Could it be that they have a common cause in a common attitude? Are they saying something about the way people think about one another, about what it means to be a human being?

Life and society in Britain in the twenty-first century are very different from what they were 50 years ago, even 20 years ago. And the change is not just down to computers, iPods and mobile phones. People are living longer, so there are more old people needing care. More babies are being born with learning disabilities in spite of screening, in part because earlier births survive, but may suffer serious damage from birth traumas. Disabled people are more likely to live into adulthood and even old age. When you add the overlay of immigration from Europe and the world trouble spots it is no wonder that the UK population is growing. And you don't need a degree in sociology to realise that this has consequences for all of us, not least in that there will be more and more people who will need care.

Sorry if I sound a bit like the proverbial 'grumpy old man', a gloomy pessimist longing for the Golden Age of my youth. We must face up to the real world in which we must live the Christian life for the glory of God.

THE SOLUTION OF SECULARISM

You have to go back nearly 100 years if you want to recall the days when most children were sent to Sunday School and church attendance was regarded as normal. That is certainly not the case today. In fact just this week I overheard a group of mature, middle-class adults talking over coffee about a friend who had started going to church. They laughed out loud at such unusual behaviour. There has been a distinct change of attitude towards religion in general and Christianity in particular. Magazine programmes on BBC Radio 4 express astonishment at anyone who believes in the possibility of creation! Interviewing of politicians, Christians and church leaders is routinely hostile - as if they were equally despicable.

We can no longer take it for granted that 'the person in the street' knows the basics of the Gospel. Nor can we assume that people who are religious will be considered acceptable company; the cases of sexual abuse by clergy and the extremism of religious terrorists have given ground for caution. In some situations wearing a Christian symbol, like a cross, is considered unacceptable, even provocative. Local authorities have even tried to change Christmas into a secular festival! A pastor may hesitate to advertise for a Christian secretary for fear of breaching employment and discrimination legislation. Like it or not this is the real world where we are to express the love of God, and we need to understand it better so that we can appreciate just how different our contribution will be. Which is why I decided to find out more about humanism.

I have to say that what I have so far learned about humanism has been at best disappointing and mostly rather depressing. You might suspect that this was because my attitude was wrong in the first place, but that is not entirely true. In spite of its outspoken atheism I somehow thought that humanism would be largely about humans, that they could offer a rationale for valuing people. If they do, then they don't make much noise about it! To be fair, the website of the British Humanist Association refers to their interest in people but the published works I have read are obsessed with something else entirely: religion and God! Stephen Law's little book, *Humanism: a Very Short Introduction,* is praised by Polly Toynbee, President of the British Humanist Association, as a 'succinct and inspiring guide to humanist thinking'. But every page of the book verges on being a blast against some aspect or other of religion. One (atheist) reviewer compared it to buying a book on vegetarianism and finding it hardly mentioned the subject because every page was given over to an attack on meat eating. In spite of this, secularism is having far more influence than the church in shaping society's attitudes today.

Twenty years ago we were trying to get to grips with existentialism when in swept post-modernism, with New Atheism riding on its coat tails. We face a more strident science which has raised speculation to the level of fact.

> Our culture is dominated by a view of human beings which derives primarily from some aspects of 17th and 18th century philosophy: rational, individualized, autonomous beings, without purpose, whose values are relative, and whose knowledge of the world is defined by what can be seen and felt and measured.[2]
>
> D ATKINSON

Science has become the new authority, and education in the broadest sense is the means by which it is promoted. And science rather than religion has become the way forward for humanity. A C Grayling, Professor of Philosophy at Birkbeck College, University of London, enthusiastically points to the importance of science:

> Science is to the contemporary world what art was to the Renaissance: a magnificent achievement that transforms humanity's perception of itself and its relationship to the world.[3]

So, in his book *What is Good?* Grayling argues that we need to promote science as the 'supreme good' as it will root us in realism, along with the study of history which will expose the atrocities committed in the name of religion and thus wean us off its myths.

The greatest happiness for the greatest number - known as utilitarianism - is widely seen by humanists as the goal for personal fulfilment but because it is so vague and impersonal few seem to have found it a practical life-style. This may be why Grayling and others are so focussed on promoting personal freedom and autonomy, for which, in their view, the abandonment of religion is essential. The idea that there is a god of any sort is considered irrational and unscientific, and the suggestion is anathema that such a god has the right to impose laws on how we should behave - and thereby restrict our freedoms.

> The real problem faced by the humanist project is the survival of religious beliefs and practices . . . All these forms of religious expression are essentially regressive, oppressive and at best medieval, and their dissonance with the modern world is a continual and too often terrible source of conflict.[4]

There is, however, a black hole at the heart of Grayling's thesis; freedom and autonomy cannot be permitted to those who wish to be free to express their faith in the public arena. Religion must be restricted to the private sphere where, without the oxygen of public acceptance, it will wither and die. So much for personal freedom?

The humanist position is always robustly expressed and there are numerous advocates. But their position is not unassailable. They rightly blame religion for dreadful atrocities in the history of our race, but they fail to face up to the equally awful atrocities of secularism wearing the guise of Communism, Stalinist and Maoist, and the horrors of fascism. Even some of their own, like Anthony Flew, have come to admit that loathing religion is no excuse for lack of intellectual integrity and have changed their position to one which at least accepts that there is a god. And there are many thorough ripostes by Bible believing writers and thinkers which show the short-comings of atheism.

We may find our faith unshaken by the atheists' assault on what we believe but we cannot ignore the way they have contributed to the change in social attitudes. The call for personal freedom and individual autonomy is to be heard whenever moral and ethical issues are in the news. Consider some examples.

Assisted suicide has been the goal of a long-running campaign. Whenever it comes to the fore we are presented with a likeable, reasonable person, often in a wheelchair, who for one reason or another wants the 'right' to be helped to die when or before their terminal condition becomes intolerable. They imply no threat to anyone else but appeal to our compassion to grant them the freedom to decide their own fate.

The same sort of thing happens with respect to so-called 'designer babies'. Parents plead for the right to select the embryo that will make this child a 'saviour sibling' to a sick or disabled brother or sister already struggling with an otherwise incurable condition. It may become yet more so with the legalisation of 'three donor babies'.

Or consider euthanasia and 'the right to die' in one's chosen manner at one's chosen time. Or abortion, or some forms of transplant surgery, or embryonic stem cell research to find cures for fear-filled diseases. Or even eugenics, which is creeping back onto some agendas.

This is not the place to discuss the arguments for or against these issues. They are mentioned to show that the way they are being discussed has changed. It is no longer in terms of principle or of right and wrong but in terms of personal freedom and popular opinion. But could it be that this very same freedom motivated the greed with which youngsters snatched designer trainers and mobile phones from the stores they attacked in London and elsewhere in 2011? Could it be that the neglect suffered by some of the old people in care was because those who were supposed to look after them were not convinced it was worth their making the effort to meet their needs?

The fact that we will want to differ from secularisms agendas does not imply that we think that Christians alone can do good or that, left to themselves, people will invariably prove uncaring and selfish. The level of altruism in society is impressive, evident in the thousands of people who give their time in voluntary work, give their money to disaster relief, and take up careers in caring professions. For every example of the public disgrace of agencies or individuals who fail those who depend on them, there are far more who, unheralded, give themselves unstintingly to maintain the highest possible levels of excellence.

THE CHRISTIAN RESPONSE

Given prevailing attitudes in society it is little wonder that many do not understand our wish to provide services of a clearly Christian character. But note the phrase, 'Christian character', not just a Christian label, as if all we are doing is adding the sign of the fish to our otherwise indistinguishable efforts. After all it is difficult to see how doing someone's shopping can somehow be Christianised. Many of the services provided by Christian organisations, be they lobbying campaigns or caring or youth work and so on, are likely to share many or most of the characteristics of services provided by those who are not motivated by faith.

In most respects Christians are almost indistinguishable from other people. They eat and drink, fall in love (and maybe out of it too), live in houses or flats, earn their living or draw appropriate benefits, pay their taxes, and play their part in society. All of this the Bible expects and regards as normal. But Christians are also expected to be different - even as they eat and drink, fall in and out of love, live in houses, earn their living etc. It is not so much a difference in what they do but who they are. They have dual nationality, dual citizenship if you prefer; they are citizens of their home country and citizens of God's kingdom. We are required by Scripture to be good citizens of our country. But we are also to fulfil the will of our Saviour and Lord who is King of kings.

Or you can look at it from another perspective: Christians belong to two communities. They belong to the community in which they live, their human community which may be expressed in a variety of contexts and networks. They also belong to another community which the New Testament calls the Body of Christ, the Church. And this in turn is on three levels, for it is both a local community and world-wide community while at the same time being a heavenly community.

Curiously, I found no reference to community in my reading on humanism. Perhaps their emphasis on the freedom and autonomy of the individual obscures their recognition of how limited we would be without one another. John Donne famously expressed this at the beginning of the seventeenth century:

> No man is an island entire to itself; every man is a piece of the Continent, a part of the main; if a clod be washed away by the sea, Europe is the less, as well as if a promontory were . . . any man's death diminishes me because I am involved in Mankind; And therefore never send to know for whom the bell tolls: it tolls for thee.[5]

A focus on autonomy has shaped the lives of people who depend on statutory services because of old age, poverty or disability. Enabling elderly people to continue living in their own homes seems a fine ideal but consigns many to aching loneliness. Supported Living for people with learning disabilities seems to them like a dream come true until their support is cut and they face hour upon hour of solitude and day-time TV.

Independence is effective when it is linked in to interdependence. Finding the right relationship between the two is part of our Christian mission.

> We are completely dependent upon God; yet in order to function faithfully and fulfil our vocation we need to develop independence that is nonetheless based upon dependence. We need to become dependently independent. The key, for Christians, is not to forget our core dependency as we strive to develop our independence. The tragedy of modernity is the way in which it has confused the story of dependent independence with the story of unfettered freedom.[6]
>
> J SWINTON

As we have already acknowledged, there are many people whose natural altruism has made them into caring and compassionate contributors to the lives of others. We applaud them for their work and admire them for their motivation. We do not imply criticism of their efforts by saying that we want to make our contribution on a different basis, one that springs out of our Christian faith. We are not out to be different by being odd-ball; our goal is to be different by being distinctive, special - or to give it a technical and theological description: holy.

What the rest of this study aims to show is that Christian motivation, values, freedom, justice and hope are all distinctive and these are the drivers which impel us forward in serving others. When the humanists tell us that our religion must be a personal and private matter they show how little they understand our faith. Our lives do not divide neatly into private and public, as if we can be one sort of person at work and a quite different person at leisure. We are as much driven by our faith as the humanist is driven by his world view and philosophy. Our relationship with God is not something we consign to a bedside cabinet before we go out to face the day and then take it out again when we get home. It is a vital part of our everyday experience and engagement with the world about us from the moment we wake to the moment we fall asleep at night. In all our living we make it our aim to walk worthy of our God and Saviour.

[1]   *Hidden from Plain Sight* p11 Report of the Equality and Human Rights Commission

[2]   David Atkinson, *The Message of Genesis* 1-11, p139

[3]   A C Grayling, *What is Good?* p244

[4]   ibid p233

[5]   John Donne, *Meditation XVII* www.quotationspage.com

[6]   Swinton, John, Mowat, Harriet and Baines, Susannah (2011) *'Whose Story Am I? Redescribing Profound Intellectual Disability in the Kingdom of God',* Journal of Religion, Disability and Health, 15:13

CHAPTER 2
A DIFFERENT SENSE OF VALUE

GOD - PRIORITY

'In the beginning God . . . .' So the Bible begins: no discussion, no explanation, no argument, no qualification. Simply assertion, a statement of fact, a summary description of reality. It is bold. It is radical; confrontational even. God is! There is nothing before him; nothing exempt from him; nothing beyond him. The familiarity of this opening statement sets its stamp on all that follows and, in a sense, shapes the Bible's expectations of its readers. God is prior and is to be priority.

For the humanist this is the wrong place to begin a discussion about human beings or, for that matter, any discussion. The assertion is irrational, with no demonstrable scientific evidence to support it and no philosophical credibility. It is a matter of superstition (or of faith, if you prefer) and is therefore to be consigned to the realm of private thought. It has no place in public practice or the social sphere.

If religion were simply a matter of philosophy it might be worth pausing to debate the question the humanist raises, but for the

Christian this is not so mundane. This is both a matter of truth and of personal relationship. We know God. It is as simple and as profound as that. We haven't always known God and the fact that we know him now is not because we became good enough to be admitted to an inner circle, nor is it because we were clever enough to understand what others could not see. But we know that we know God, that he is our Father and our Friend.

Secularism simply does not 'get it', this matter of relationship with God, because it refuses to acknowledge the very existence of God, let alone his priority. So it assumes that we Christians behave as we do because we are oppressed by a set of rules imposed by a mythical being 'out there'. It imagines us cowed with fear by some tyrannical deity waiting to strike us for any misdemeanour or hoping that our pathetic efforts will gain us a toehold in some future existence. They could hardly be more mistaken. Which is why the Christian approach to human worth is radically different from what they expect it to be, and from their own propositions.

From the Christian's perspective God cannot be relegated to some personal, private corner of our lives, a sort of inoffensive bolt-on to help us through our personal inadequacies. Knowing God is the corner-stone of life for us, as real and at least as important as our relationship with our spouse or closest friend. For that is what it is: a relationship. We set off for work in the morning, moving from the private to the public sphere, but we remain friends or husbands or wives or fathers or mothers or sons or daughters. Indeed it is at least in part because of those relationships that we venture out of our comfort zone to demanding jobs and situations. We may also continue to wear the symbols of those relationships: the wedding ring, that tie from a much loved daughter, or the bags under the eyes from the night-calls of a newborn child! They serve as reminders to others as much as ourselves of the people we love. And those relationships will qualify the other relationships we have during the course of the day. That is how it is for Christians in their relationship with God. It will be as real on the factory floor as in church, as real sitting in a traffic jam as in the quiet corner where we read our Bible. Whether in public or in private, knowing God will be important for the believer because it is real. Not only is knowing God real for the Christian, it is also deeply reasonable. To dismiss it as irrational is to miss the fact that our faith is rooted in history. Every key truth finds its basis or its echo in real events that took place in real time in real places

A Christian's relationship with God is bound to affect the way they live and it is different from the way they lived before becoming a Christian. The Bible has various metaphors to express this difference. It depicts the Christian as a citizen of another kingdom, as a member of God's family, as belonging to a spiritual community and so on. This can seem strange, even threatening to those who are not believers. Some Roman emperors regarded it as treasonable. Modern China has regarded it as subversive, and atheists think it deluded. But for the Christian, knowing God has priority in every sphere of life. It is the primary consideration in every decision.

This then is the basis on which we consider how we who are Christians should live in the world. We respond to the challenges and opportunities to show the love and care of God for the people who live around us, especially those who, for whatever reason, we recognise to be disadvantaged.

IMAGE - PERSONHOOD

'What is man?' (Ps 8:4) It is an old, old question. King David posed it some 3,000 years ago and it is doubtful that he was the first to do so; he certainly was not the last. It reverberates through philosophy from Ancient Greece to the present day. And it has produced some memorable, much admired and oft repeated answers. Here is Protagorus from the fifth century BC: 'Man is the measure of all things'. It sounds profound and impressive, if somewhat self-important. But does it help us towards an answer to the question? Is it even credible? How can a creature as small as a human being be in any way the measure of the immensity of the universe? Can a being so finite, so temporary, influence to any significant degree the movements of time and space whose rhythms regulate his world?

Descartes (1596-1650) 'set out to make belief in God invulnerable to sceptical assault'.[1] Along the way he offered his answer to King David's question: 'I think therefore I am'. Again one is impressed by the brevity and seeming profundity of his aphorism, but it sheds little light on what or who we are. One is left wondering whether the demented old lady who is now beyond thinking, or the new-born baby whose only responses are instinctual, can be said even to exist on Descartes' thesis. The question still demands an answer.

What does it mean to be human? Indeed what is a human being? Why, in spite of evolutionism on the one hand and experiments on human embryos on the other, do we feel special? What marks us out from every other life form on the planet? There are primates that look (vaguely?) like us, birds that talk, dogs that fetch newspapers, creatures that can walk on two legs, but we feel that we are different to a profound degree, not merely a further development of what they are or can do. What is it that makes people, people?

Answering this question is likely to be the major moral and ethical issue facing us in the twenty-first century. Many of the already significant moral challenges have this as their root question: should we permit assisted suicide, experiments on embryos, saviour siblings, spare part surgery, 'paid for' organs for transplant, remunerated surrogacy, not to mention euthanasia, human genetic manipulation, gender selection, human cloning - and doubtless many other procedures not yet imagined?

The answers to all such questions will reflect what we think about human-ness. It is an issue for us as individuals but it also confronts Christian organisations and churches. We and they will be called upon to express and defend our convictions concerning many of the contemporary moral issues as they relate to human needs, rights and obligations.

So many issues are raised by the questions surrounding our human-ness that we need an organising principle which will hold our answers together in a consistent manner. Such a principle has to achieve at least the following:

- It must include everything that needs to be included.
- It must be universally true.

Our explanation as to what defines us as human beings must include every human being - male and female, young and old, rich and poor, clever and not so clever, tall and short, fat and thin, every colour and skin shade, regardless of religion, philosophy or creed. Our principle needs to be true whether we are talking of Englishmen in Birmingham or Bahrain, or Russians in Moscow or Morocco; whether we are discussing a seminar in a top university or the reception class in a special school. There is no room for favouritism here. Christianity must produce a principle which meets the criteria in full. It must fit the way things are and the way we feel about them: that human beings are significant in a way animals are not - no disrespect to the cat; that we are more than the body in which we live; that we are not simply some sort of biological machine. The principle must also take account of our awareness of the divine, indeed it cannot fail to do so.

Thankfully such a principle exists, and the very first chapter of the Bible begins to unfold it for us. There is no need for us to be side-tracked by the big questions raised by science and scientism at this point. Whatever our view on the creation/evolution issue, we can make two firm statements about the early chapters of Genesis. First, they were never intended to be scientific description of our origins. Second, what they reveal to us is, as Francis Schaeffer described it, 'true truth'. They are not the trance-induced ramblings of some ancient shaman-type leader, or mere fairy tales handed down through centuries as folklore What we find in Genesis chapter one provides the clearest and firmest basis for understanding what we are. Here is our organising principle:

> Then God said, 'Let us make man in our image, in our likeness . . . .' So God created man in his own image, in the image of God he created him; male and female he created them. (Gen 1:26,27)

As James Packer comments on these verses:

> The repetition is, of course, for emphasis, as in all human language; the story is drumming into us that our dignity as bearers of God's image is the first thing about ourselves that we need to grasp.[2]

Hold on to that. It is the key to everything which follows in human history. It is God's breathtaking organising principle by which we can discover what we are and why we are. The very idea that human beings - ie, male and female - are made in God's image would have been audacious if it had been dreamed up by Moses or conjured by the apostle Paul. This is God's explanation of the distinction between ourselves and the rest of creation.

> The concept of the image of God is at the heart of Christian anthropology.[3]
>
> A A HOEKEMA

At this point some may feel that we are in too much of a hurry. The story of our creation is quickly followed by the account of Adam and Eve's disobedience and ejection from the Garden of Eden. That changed everything, they assert. Not entirely; the Bible continues to speak of human beings as made in God's image both specifically and, by implication, right through into the New Testament.

> The image of God as such is an unlosable aspect of man, a part of his essence and existence, something that man cannot lose without ceasing to be man.[4]
>
> A A HOEKEMA

At times the Bible makes statements are breathtaking, as when King David answered his own question as to the nature of human beings. The former shepherd boy was probably remembering those crystal clear nights on the hillside when the stars illumined the darkness from one horizon to another. Anyone who has witnessed the scene away from the light pollution of our cities and towns will understand David's sense of awe:

> When I consider your heavens, the work of your fingers, the moon and the stars, which you have set in place, what is man that you are mindful of him? (Ps 8:3,4)

We are dwarfed by the vastness of the universe. How can we possibly claim to be significant? The wonder that the psalmist expresses for us is that we human beings are incredibly significant. He continues:

> You made him a little lower than the heavenly beings and crowned him with glory and honour. You made him ruler of the works of your hands. (Ps 8:5,6)

The psalm then goes on to describe how God gave responsibility for the natural world to humankind, further underlining how important we are in his plan of things. In fact when we look at these verses more closely this becomes overwhelmingly clear. Most English translations seem reluctant to render the Hebrew literally. You may find in the margin of your Bible a note which gives an alternative reading for 'heavenly beings' as 'than God'. If you then put the sentence together again it will read like this:

> What is man that you are mindful of him . . . You made him a little lower than God.

That seems to us an exaggeration, but that is exactly what the psalmist discovered and it takes us right back to the Garden of Eden - and on to the final resurrection! It is this startling fact that makes human beings valuable: we are God-like.

This is in stark contrast to the kind of theology which emphasises the darker statements of Scripture about human nature. Great and godly men and women of Scripture were often painfully aware of their unworthiness. Jeremiah cried out that 'the heart is deceitful above all things and beyond cure'. (Jer 17:9) Isaiah bewailed his uncleanness. (Isa 6:5) Peter was so aware of his sin that he asked Jesus to go away and leave him alone. (Lk 5:8) Paul spoke of himself as the worst of sinners. (1 Tim 1:15) This wasn't false humility on their part. It is true that we human beings are incorrigibly sinful. It is our natural bent, our preferred outlet. Theologians describe this as 'total depravity', not meaning by that that we are all as bad as we could be, but that sinfulness naturally penetrates to every aspect of our human-ness. 'There is no-one righteous, not even one' (Rom 3:10) is not an accusation; it is a simple statement of fact. All this feels a long way from the glories of Psalm 8 and the potential of Eden. We need to look more closely at what the Bible means when it describes human beings as bearing God's image.

As soon as we ask how or what the image of God in people is we step into a vast field of discussion (and speculation?) which has occupied theologians for centuries! That in itself should alert us to the fact that we cannot be certain, but at the same time we need to glean what we can from what the Bible says as it is clearly a key issue. The place to start is in Eden. In Genesis 1:26,27 the words 'image' and 'likeness' are translations of two different Hebrew words. The differences between them are slight and they are used interchangeably in Scripture, but there are differences. One seems to relate to what a human being is and the other to what people do because of who they are. So every person is in some way to mirror God and thereby is able to represent God on earth. Human beings are in some way like God and because of this are able to act like God - God-likeness and godliness. At the Fall our ability to act like God and represent him was damaged, but God-like characteristics remained; godliness was still a possibility.

In what ways, then, are human beings like God? The first clues are found in Genesis 1:26, 'Then God said, "Let us make man in our image ..."' In the sequence of creation this is the first time God proposes to use himself as the pattern of what he will make - the man and the woman. This obviously involves the fact that, since God is spirit, human beings will have spiritual faculties. But there is something at least as significant: God is plural; this is the first hint of the trinity, a theme to be more fully developed in the New Testament. God acted in relationship in creating human beings as those who would live in relationships. Almost before you turn the page from Genesis 1 you read what God says of the solitary man: 'It is not good for the man to be alone'. (Gen 2:18) Woman is to be as much and as important a part of the human story as the man.

We are God-like in our capacity for relationship. We were made to be social beings, able to develop and enjoy a range of relationships which are without parallel in the creation. Some aspects of it are mirrored in animals and birds, but the richness possible through love and language and learning between human beings results in relationships which are far and away beyond anything all other creatures can experience. We were made for relationship with God our Maker. We were also made for relationships with other people; we cannot be fully human in isolation! And we were also made to relate to the world around us, to develop its potential, to serve and nurture it for the benefit of all creation. There is nothing else in all that God has made capable of experiencing and fulfilling such rich relationships.

> In Biblical thought, humanity is defined not so much by
> rationality as by relationality.[5]
>
> J WYATT

In addition there are many other characteristics in human beings which reflect God:

- We have moral faculties which are innate and unlearned, though clearly inhibited by our preference for sin. (Rom 2:14,15) For some this is a 'first order' issue: 'Moral personhood is the real centre of our likeness to God, and his to us.'[6] J PACKER

- We are able to think rationally, to develop ideas, to make decisions, to reflect upon our lives.

- We are able to appreciate beauty, to be creative, to communicate through a range of arts and language.

- We are able to laugh!

The degree to which one or other of the characteristics is present does not affect the degree to which a person is more, or less, human. If that were so then we might argue that a criminal was less of a man than a detective is; an artist might be more human than a mathematician; a shy girl might be less human than a brash boy - and so on.

This `image' concept is something which is universally true. It includes people of all sorts and sizes, colours and creeds, races and regions. And at the same time it excludes whatever is not human. The queen bee may rule the hive but her reign does not extend beyond it. The buzzard may draw a circle in the air but is no artist.

> It may be, however, that it is beyond us to conceive the full essence of the image, not only because we cannot grasp all that God is, but also because we are so largely mysterious to ourselves, being ignorant of the depths of our own fallen and disordered natures. Perhaps, therefore, we should limit ourselves to saying that the dignity of humanity lies in a God-likeness which doubtless has more to it than we can know in any single case, least of all our own.[7]
>
> J PACKER

So there you have our organising principle, our answer to the question what and who are we as human beings. People are made in the image of God, albeit marred by sin. This principle in every way satisfies our search for something which is universally true and relevant. It recognises all the faults, flaws and failings in people but at the same time says of them: 'You are wonderful!'

VALUE - PRECIOUS

Some time ago *The Times* published a poster for children entitled: 'What are you made of?' It illustrated the chemical content of the human body. Did you know that the average person's body has as much carbon as 9,000 pencil leads, enough uranium (0.1mg) to power a 100w light bulb for 10 minutes, as much potassium (140g) as 333 bananas, as much calcium (1kg) as 1,450 pints of skimmed milk, as much fluorine (2.6g) as is in 26 tubes of toothpaste and even 1.2mg of gold (worth one penny)? Our bones weigh as much as an elephant's tusk and we have as much fat as 35 large packs of butter (though I suspect there is some variation in this statistic!). It was an engaging way to teach children, but it leaves a question hanging in the air: if that is what I am, is that all I am worth?

Secularism struggles with the concept of human value. In an industrial age it tended to think in terms of productivity. Even children were sucked into the mines and mills to add to the profit of the company. It was eventually seen for what it was - the exploitation of those whose energy and skill it drained. Today it seems that celebrity is most highly valued. Protests at the enrichment of bankers and captains of industry seem inconsistent when no such protest is raised at the salaries paid to footballers, sportsmen and film stars.

What of those who are not productive, glamorous, gifted, creative, industrious, and successful? What about the ordinary Joes - and Janes - who share our bus queue and supermarket aisles? Are they worth less? What of the man struggling with the onset of dementia, the woman suffering from cancer, the youngster frustrated by dyslexia, the quadriplegic former soldier limbless through conflict - have they no value? Or the homeless vagrant, the drop-out, the unemployed and seemingly unemployable? There are tens of thousands, millions even, who do not rate on most value systems, are they to be dismissed? Our gut instinct is to say no, but why not?

> From the secular point of view it is hard to explain why we feel as we do about this, since on secular principles it is impossible, finally, to isolate anything about us that should entitle us to such precedence or privilege over all other living creatures on our planet.[8]
>
> J PACKER

Whatever other people think, whatever current philosophies say, whatever the ups and downs of life may suggest, we intuitively act and think as if we have supreme value.[9]

OS GUINESS

C S Lewis put it more bluntly: 'There are no ordinary people. You have never met a "mere mortal".'[10]

The Bible teaches that, behind and beyond appearances, our very human-ness makes every one of us incalculably valuable. People have value because of what they are as God's image bearers. And it was because of this distinctive that the Son of God could become a human being and actually did so in space-time history. The incarnation is a fact. God could not have become an animal of any sort because there is nothing in animals (even lions!) which can connect with deity in the way humanity can. But the incarnation is more than a fact: it is a marvellous declaration of value, a hallmark of incredible significance. More than this: the Son of God was not only born as a human being but was born into a poor family, to grow up in all the ordinariness of a carpenter's home and workshop. When he began his life's work on earth it was to face scorn for his humble background, mockery for his lack of education and rejection of all he stood for. The further humiliation was to suffer unwarranted arrest, an unjust trial and illegal execution as a common criminal. As if all that were not enough he suffered the punishment due to us for our sins - he was 'made sin for us'. It is a mark of God's great love that Jesus went through this for us but it was more than that: it was a declaration of how precious we are to him. The reason that God was 'manifest in the flesh' is itself a statement of how much God values people. As Peter wrote:

> For you know that it was not with perishable things such as silver or gold that you were redeemed from the empty way of life handed down to you from your forefathers, but with the precious blood of Christ. (1Pet 1:18)

The New Testament repeatedly reminds us of the cost of our salvation, which in turn tells us how precious human beings are to God. Certainly 'worth more than many sparrows'. (Luke 12:7) Which is why God is committed to restoring the shattered likeness to its original form. Those who believe in Jesus are being 'transformed into his likeness'. (2 Cor 3:18)

In moral debates one will often hear arguments based on 'the sanctity of life'. Most of us have some idea what is meant by this but it is hard to explain and does not make a strong case simply because it is so abstract. We feel that life is special and to be protected, particularly in human beings! The Bible sets down a much firmer foundation for us to speak up for the unborn and the vulnerable because it puts a value on human life which is rooted in the character of God. People are to be valued simply because they are people. Because a person's worth does not depend on what they can do, how productive they can be, how well they can argue their own case, let alone how much they have in the bank: we are obliged to value them however much or little they have or can contribute to society.

There has been an attack on such an inclusive principle in recent years by those who argue that personhood should only be acknowledged in those who are capable of certain functions. Even being born to human parents is not considered sufficient by some. Prof Peter Singer of Princeton University (and author of 'Should the Baby Live? The problem of handicapped infants' in 1985) may be an extreme example of this but he is also very influential. He argues that before a baby is recognised as a human being it should show evidence of faculties which are widespread in the human race. And this recognition cannot be granted until the newborn reaches a certain age which, though young, would permit both infanticide and abortion as a matter of course. It would require some 'body' to determine what the standard for acceptance into the human society should be. He goes further to argue that a person with disabilities is to be valued less than a non-disabled person. Those he calls 'mental defectives' may be used for scientific experimentation.[11] They may even be worth less than animals! Evidence of Singer's continuing influence was seen by the publication on the website of the British Medical Journal of an article[12] by Ablerto Giubilini and Francesca Minerva advocating what they called 'after-birth abortion'. It is the ultimate devaluing of personhood. It is also the inevitable logic of evolutionism.

The Christian perspective generates a theology of diversity. It recognises ability and lack of ability as much in one group of people as in any other. Just as one person might be a manager and another a musician so the widest possible range of gifts lies open to be utilised, recognising that mutual support is part and parcel of life for every individual, not just those who have 'disabilities'. The outcomes will be altogether more positive, more fulfilling for a larger number of people. It will parallel with the New Testament picture of the Church as the Body of Christ, where every part has it function and 'those parts of the body that seem to be weaker are indispensable'. (1 Cor 12:22)

Prospects crystallised its understanding of the practical demands of valuing people with learning disability in its Principle of Personal Value. During a training course to equip people for ministry among people with learning disabilities one participant commented with some surprise, 'But this applies to all of us.' Quite so!

- Individuality - Each person should be valued and affirmed as an individual and enabled to express and develop their God-given uniqueness.

- Empowerment - People should be free to initiate choices and at all times be enabled to participate in decisions which affect their lives.

- Spirituality - People have spiritual needs and the right to spiritual fulfilment. They should have the opportunity for personal spiritual growth.

- Dignity - People should be valued and respected with due acknowledgement of their age and life experience.

- Independence - People should be encouraged and supported to move towards greater independence and should determine their lifestyle choices.

- Inclusion - People should be free to participate in their local and wider communities and be encouraged to understand their rights and responsibilities as citizens.[13]

This is a principle rather than a series of principles. It is only as all the elements work together that the full value of people is expressed. Furthermore any suggestion that these are rights 'we' grant to 'them' runs counter to the spirit of the principle. It is true for all persons so that no one is superior to others with power to permit them to be human!

The Christian doctrine of human-ness is far from being the strait-jacket of the parody of religion popularised by the media. It is unparalleled in its power to restore a sense of dignity and freedom to people of all sorts, at all levels of society, whatever their abilities, race or culture. Every one is to be valued.

EXPECTATION - POTENTIAL

Don't you sometimes wish the Bible told you just a bit more than it does? If only we had more detail about what it was like for Adam and Eve when they lived in the Garden of Eden. If only they had passed on how different they were before and after the Fall! However we are not left without help. We do have a well documented account of the only life not damaged or limited by sin ever to be lived on earth. The life of Jesus shows what God's image in a human being can be like. He was 'the exact representation of his (God's) being'. (Heb 1:3) When Philip, one of Jesus' disciples, struggled to understand what God the Father is like, Jesus said to him, 'Anyone who has seen me has seen the Father.' (Jn 14:9) Paul makes several similar statement in several of his letters.

> Though God is invisible, in Christ the invisible God becomes visible; one who looks at Christ is actually looking at God.[14]
>
> A A HOEKEMA

By studying the life and ministry of Jesus as described and explained in the New Testament we gain a strong impression of what could have been if our first parents had not sinned. We are able to understand a little of the great loss the human race, and indeed the whole of creation, has suffered as a consequence of disobeying our Maker. The impact has been disastrous. But the situation is not hopeless, for the message of the Gospel, the reason for God becoming a human being in Christ, is to reverse the results of the Fall both in those who believe in the Saviour, and also, ultimately, in the whole of creation.

The New Testament indicates that someone who believes in Christ can be progressively changed to become more and more like the ideal person, the Lord Jesus Christ himself. At conversion the believer becomes a new person, receives the Holy Spirit into their life, and then begins a process of transformation (theologically described as sanctification) which reaches it fulfilment when, at death, they become finally and fully like Christ. They then take their place in the heavenly company of all who, like them, have trusted in the Lord Jesus Christ. [15]

The relevance of this 'eschatological' dimension is that our involvement with people will begin with their immediate circumstances and real personal needs but will also look beyond that to what they could be and what they will become - in time and eternity. It will enable us to regard people as of value because of their unrealised potential as well as in the light of their unique creation. We will see our duty not only in terms of alleviating present difficulties but also in enabling and empowering the person's fullest possible fulfilment in the future.

Different? The contrast between the Christian approach to the value of every person has no parallel in any other philosophy or religion. It provides us with a comprehensive and inclusive approach to everyone, without regard to their background, present situation or condition. Unqualified acceptance of a person's worth is integral to our faith and therefore must determine every aspect of our response to them. Yes, it is different, and it is demanding, but if we take Jesus as our example then, like him, we will be committed to give expression to this dynamic truth at every opportunity. And like him, we will find ourselves drawn to those for whom the need to be valued is the greatest. However, could this prove to be a threat to our freedom and autonomy?

1. Alister McGrath *The Twilight of Atheism* p31

2. James Packer & Thomas Howard *Christianity, The True Humanism* p138

3. Anthony A Hoekema *Created in God's Image* p66

4. Ibid p32

5. John Wyatt, *Matters of Life and Death* p52

6. Packer & Howard p140

7. Ibid p143

8. Ibid p138

9. Os Guinness, *The Call,* p18

10. C S Lewis quoted by John Blanchard in *Does God believe in Atheists* p324

11. From John Blanchard, *Does God believe in Atheists,* p369

12. A Giubilini and F Minerva, *After-birth abortion: why should the baby live?* published online www.jme.bmj.com, March 2, 2012

13. This is an adaptation of the PPV, as it is normally expressed within Prospects in terms of people with learning disabilities.

14. A A Hoekema, op cit p21

15. See 2 Cor 5:17, 2 Cor 3:18, Eph 4:13,23, Col 3:10, 1 Jn 3:2

CHAPTER 3
A DIFFERENT SENSE OF FREEDOM

Freedom! the cry of slaves and oppressed peoples down the millennia which still echoes in the streets and squares of Egypt and Libya and Syria and in the alleyways of Tibet. Freedom! with the sun on your face and the wind in your hair, with deadlines and timetables forgotten for a few precious days of holiday. Freedom! in the realisation of all the 'if only's' of our dreams and aspirations. Everyone is in favour of freedom, at least for themselves and those close to them.

Humanism has almost made freedom its campaign slogan: every person free and autonomous. And it is catching on: our increasingly secular society rises to the idea, showing its enthusiasm for freedom in its demand for human rights. We will return to the issue of human rights in the next chapter but for now we note the way in which we all expect them to be honoured even when we are not entirely sure what they are. And when we hear of an illegal immigrant not being deported on 'human rights' grounds because he has a cat, we begin to wonder if things may have gone too far.

For humanists the near universal and unchallenged acceptance of the rights agenda is encouraging. When they express the view that human beings should be free and autonomous they are not primarily thinking of slavery or oppression, however. Their goal is to set people free from an externally imposed morality - imposed, that is, by a god who will punish any deviation from his rules. It is up to us to decide what is right and wrong. We should live the good life because we know it to be good rather than out of fear of judgement or damnation or in order to get an entry ticket to heaven. It might seem to you just a bit risky to let everyone do their own thing, but humanists describe such a world in near utopian language. Here is A C Grayling's concluding sentence in his book, *What is Good? The search for the best way to live*:

> To the question "What is good?", then, the answer can only be: "The considered life - free, creative, informed and chosen, a life of achievement and fulfilment, of pleasure and understanding, of love and friendship; in short, the best human life in a human world, humanely lived." [1]

You almost feel you should stand for a fanfare! However, had you read from the beginning of the book you would more likely hear the sound of hot air escaping! The humanist dream of a god-free future turns out to be less impressive.

The world won't work without laws. Humanists know that as well as anyone. The whole universe functions as well as it does because of forces we do not see and barely understand. Nothing is completely 'free'. The stars that seem to move so freely across the night sky, the seagull that soars above the cliff with barely a wing-beat, the wind that rustles the leaves - all are held in their stillness and their movement by constraints we call 'natural laws'. Whether it is the astronaut looking out from his space capsule or the researcher peering down her microscope, what they see is ordered, interdependent and predictable. We are spectators of forces and facts beyond our knowing. We are not surprised by this order, but when it malfunctions we are frightened and awed - whether it is a tsunami or an erupting volcano.

What we see in nature we see also in human experience. All our 'freedoms' are subject to laws and constraints. You hear a pianist play a melody that touches your deepest emotion, perhaps with joy, or sadness, or wonder. You envy her ability to turn emotion into liquid sound. Yet you know that, however spontaneously her fingers seem to flow over the keys, what you hear is the result of hour after hour of dull, determined discipline. So are the ballet dancer's fluid movements, and the athlete's speed, and the scientist's ground-breaking discovery.

The world works because of order and constraints both at the level of 'nature' and human experience. If it is also to work at the level of society and community there must similarly be order and constraint. We need a moral framework. The Christian and the humanist are at one on this, but they differ as to how that moral framework is determined and of what it consists. That leads to marked differences concerning what is right and wrong - or, as they might express it, what is the good life.

For the humanist the search for morality must begin with a denial: it is not given by a god. As the quote from A C Grayling showed, it must be human in its origin and its expression. Of that there is no vagueness, but the more one reads the humanist case the more one is unsure just what is right and wrong - for at the end of the day that is what we need to know if our lives are to be good. The nearest they come to an answer is with utilitarianism, also known as consequentialism.

> This theory holds that right actions are those which produce the greatest total pleasure for everyone affected by their consequences and wrong actions are those which fail to produce this greatest total pleasure.[2]

Not all humanists accept utilitarianism. Some advocate a qualified form of this view, but all accept that human beings have a natural sense of

right and wrong and that they can determine moral questions
for themselves.

> Each individual has inevitably to rely on their own individual
> moral compass - their own sense of right and wrong - in
> weighing up to whom they should listen and whether to accept
> the moral advice they are given.[3]
>
> S LAW

A few pages later the same writer adds:

> Yes, humanist morality is very much focussed on we humans
> (and other sentient species), but that is not to say that right
> and wrong are whatever individual humans, or even human
> communities, say they are.[4]

So how are we to determine these important issues?

> Humanists emphasise the role of reason in making moral
> judgements. They believe we have a duty to apply our powers
> of reason as best we can when addressing moral questions.'[5]
>
> S LAW

Isn't this going to result in relativism, where 'everyone does what is
right in their own eyes'? Definitely not!

> The humanist's commitment to the importance of applying
> reason to moral questions clearly involves a rejection of the
> relativist view that moral truth is whatever we say it is.[6]
>
> S LAW

Just as you think you see a glimmer of light he adds:

> That is not to say that humanists suppose reason alone is capable
> of determining the answer to any moral conundrum.[7]

And so on! In short locating or describing humanist morality is rather like trying to nail down water!

The Bible's approach to moral law has been widely misunderstood - even by its supporters. Christianity, we are told, is too negative, preoccupied with 'thou shalt nots'. People want to be free! Properly understood those 'thou shalt nots' of the Ten Commandments are extraordinarily positive: they are signposts to freedom. Take the issue of sex, for example. There is one commandment about sex and that concerns the abuse of our sexuality. That is what it forbids and all that it forbids. The implication of this is that, within the boundaries set elsewhere in Scripture, we are free to enjoy what God has made for our pleasure and fulfilment. And on the issue of relationships - with parents and neighbours in particular - we are given guidance about what to avoid so that we can get on with one another in society. The commandments are not a cage to hem us in but a fence along the cliff-top to keep us from harm. Viewed like this they open up a wealth of rich possibilities for fulfilled living. We must affirm loudly and clearly that God's law is for our good as human beings. James actually describes it as 'the law of liberty' (KJV), or 'the perfect law that gives freedom.' (NIV) (James 1:25)

When we argue that God's law is the way to the 'good life' that humanists advocate we must avoid the suggestion that the only people who do good, therefore, are Christians. The vast majority of people involved in voluntary and charitable work in the UK are not consciously modelling themselves on the example of Jesus or acting out of religious motivation. Altruism is still alive and well! The point of this discussion is to show that the Christian way is different and that it freely embraces doing good as a response to God and his law. Christian voluntary and charitable work may look very similar to that of those who profess no faith but it is neither altruistic nor philanthropic. It is motivated by something else and expressive of something else. For the Christian, and admittedly it does seem paradoxical, obedience is the very expression of freedom.

If ever there was a human being who was truly free it was Jesus Christ, the Son of God. He stepped outside the morass of regulation beloved of religious leaders of his day and walked tall as a man among men. But, interestingly, he willingly took the role of a servant. When people were talking of him as a leader, even a king figure, he spoke of his mission in different terms. 'The Son of Man did not come to be served but to serve, and to give his life . . .' (Mk 10:45); 'I am among you as one who serves.' (Lk 22:27) The accounts of his life and ministry illustrate the fact: he served others - people who were poor, outcast, insignificant, unclean, disreputable, helpless. Where he saw a need he responded to it with his help and his love. Even among his own followers he was a servant, the only one in the room prepared to wash the feet of his friends. Not because of a crushing fear of judgement, or a resented obligation, or an imposed duty but because he was free of all such and had chosen to follow this path wherever it led - even though it took him to the cross. And even in his death - he was not killed - he 'laid down his life'. (Jn 10:18)

> We find ourselves presented, then, in the life of Jesus with the extreme oddity of complete obedience apparently issuing in complete freedom.[8]
>
> J PACKER

The Bible gives us a clue as to the source of Jesus' sense that he was free to serve and it does so just at the point of introducing the most outstanding example of humble service - washing the feet of his friends. 'Jesus knew that the Father had put all things under his power, and that he had come from God and was returning to God; so he got up . . . wrapped a towel around his waist . . .'(Jn 13:3,4) Notice that little word 'so'; it is making the connection: this resulted in that. Because he

knew who he was and understood why he was, he could break with
convention and simply do what was good and right, not to impress but
to teach: 'I have given you an example . . .'

Of course Jesus was different, profoundly different, from us; but he
was like us too. His personal security was in knowing who he was in
God; ours is in knowing who we are in Christ. We have been brought
into our relationship with him by God's grace. Our sins have been
forgiven. We have been given a new life with the gift of the Holy
Spirit. We are God's children by adoption. Our eternal life has begun
already. We are not trying to impress God with how good we are, nor
are we trying to earn enough Brownie points to gain our free pass into
heaven in due course. Our past is dealt with and our future is assured.

How will we use our freedom? This is so much more than the dilemma
faced by every hostage released by his captors, every prisoner who has
served his sentence, every person reaching retirement, every holiday
maker arriving at their chosen destination. The New Testament is very
clear on the matter: we can now live as free men and women and, like
Jesus, we can, as Paul puts it, 'live a life of love'. (Eph 5:1)

Here is Paul again:

> You were called to be free. But do not use your freedom to
> indulge the sinful nature; rather serve one another in love.
> The entire law is summed up in a single command: 'love your
> neighbour as yourself.' (Gal 5:13,14)

Freedom and law get married, and the knot is tied by love!

It used to strike me as odd that love is commanded: surely love is a
spontaneous response to another person. Loving someone because
they may be poor or hungry or destitute feels more like pity - and even
the desperate don't welcome that. But agape love, that distinctively

Christian word in the language of the New Testament, is a love of the will 'which operates where there is neither attraction or reciprocation'.[10] This love is not some romantic feeling, but a deep desire for the well-being of others, wanting the best for others whoever they are. It is God's love in us.

> Not love as a generally diffused feeling of warmth and good will, but as sharing in the very nature of God.[9]
>
> J PACKER

Like God's love, this has to be practical, as demonstrated and encouraged by Jesus both by his teaching and by his example. What is most striking is that it was always evident with reference to people in need. The beggar by the roadside stopped Jesus in his tracks with his plea for help. The woman who, as an outcast, interrupted him on a mission of mercy was given patient, personal attention. The terrifying madman waving his broken chains found a new and healthful beginning after meeting with Jesus. Even when he went to the home of rich Zacchaeus it was in order to mend a broken life. As he ate in the home of a wealthy Pharisee his concern was for a woman who wanted to start afresh after her life of shame. Similarly his parables mocked the games the religious people played at the expense of the poor. It was the despised 'sinners' whom Jesus befriended.

> Now the rule, or pattern, for our human life and hence for human freedom, says Christianity, is the rule of love. This is the will of God who called us into being. The point is, God is love, and we are made in his image; which means we have been made to live as he lives, doing at our level what he does at his . . . It is in the moral image of this God that we mortals were created. We have been made to love him, to be loved by him, and to love each other. Our true freedom is found in doing this.[10]
>
> J PACKER

Aren't you moved by the wonder of this, the sense that here is the way of living that is completely reasonable and explains to our heads what we know to be true in our hearts? Yet at the same time there is the recognition of the enormous privilege that is ours to reflect to an often dark world something of what God is like. What looks to the sceptic as the heavy burden of 'ought' becomes in James's lovely phrase, 'the perfect law that gives freedom'. (Jas 1:25) But it is more than a matter of doing what we are told.

[1]   A C Grayling, 'What is Good?' p249

[2]   The New Dictionary of Christian Ethics and Pastoral Theology p253

[3]   Stephen Law, 'Humanism: A very short introduction' p79

[4]   ibid p91

[5]   ibid p89

[6]   ibid p91

[7]   ibid p89

[8]   J Packer and Thomas Howard, 'Christianity: the true humanism' p63

[9]   ibid p61

[10] ibid p66/7

CHAPTER 4
A DIFFERENT SENSE OF JUSTICE

If you like a good love story then the Bible has several for your enjoyment - and instruction, of course. They are many and varied. Some are sad, like David's illicit love for Bathsheba, or Samson's for Delilah, both ending in tragedy. Some are inspiring, like the loyal love between Jonathan and David or Mary Magdalene for Jesus. But surely the story told in the Old Testament book of Ruth must be among the most beautiful, with a real 'happily ever after' ending and a significance that reaches forward to the coming of the Messiah. Read it again and notice the multi-racial, cross-cultural love and the many love-relationships.

To understand the story of Ruth fully some insight into the curious cultural and legal obligations of the Jews of that period must be understood. One instance of this was the way reapers were encouraged to be inefficient when gathering the harvest. They were deliberately to leave some of the crop for local poor people to gather for themselves. It was a custom enshrined in legislation which dated back hundreds of years to the time of Moses. (Lev 19:9,10) This simple humanitarian measure is at the heart of the Biblical concept of justice, and sets the tone for our study of the subject.

Justice is usually recognised as taking two forms: one is retributive justice, i.e. the punishment of wrong doing; the other is distributive justice, ie. the protection and granting of rights. Both Christians and humanists agree that society must deal with violations of law appropriately. They diverge, however, when it comes to the issue of distributive justice, as to the attitudes and motivations of the 'human rights agenda', and it is this difference of outlook which distinguishes their respective responses to those who are dependent or vulnerable.

A leaflet from the local Liberal Democrat councillors dropped through the door this week. It declared in bold print, 'Access to justice is a fundamental right of all citizens and the Liberal Democrats will continue to fight to protect this . . .' The same sentiment could have been expressed by any of the political parties and we would expect it of them - today. Fifty, twenty, years ago such a statement might have surprised us. The vocabulary of human rights has only become pervasive in relatively recent times. Since the Second World War the issue has steadily grown in importance with an increasing impact on legislation and on our understanding of justice. (See Appendix C for an overview of human rights and the Government's list of what rights we have.)

This development reflects the increased acceptance of secularism with its strong focus on individual freedom and autonomy. The self-assertiveness which lays claim to 'my rights' is a natural outcome. The rights themselves are not the problem; they are what one might reasonably expect of a civilised society in the twenty-first century. It is the notion of rights rather than the rights themselves which becomes problematic. Politicians have made valiant efforts to argue for a parallel agenda of responsibilities, along the lines that we cannot expect our rights from society unless we also fulfil our duties to society. It is hardly a doctrine to set the heather alight!

> In a secular society . . . responsibility is the respectable way to
> talk about morals without talking about religion . . . When we are
> called to be responsible for too much and responsible to no one,
> then responsibility itself collapses.[1]

OS GUINESS

Unsurprisingly, people are more enthusiastic to know what is their due
than what they must do. So the balance has become skewed in favour
of rights, with a Commission to enforce them and a compensation
culture to exploit any failure to observe them.

The Christian is uncomfortable with the human rights emphasis for
two reasons. First of all, the very self-assertiveness sits awkwardly with
the Bible's teaching about humility and unselfishness. It just doesn't
feel right, even when a person's claim may be legitimate. The Bible
seems to give contradictory examples. Jesus was assertive when he
spoke out, and even struck out, at the demands and practices of Jewish
leaders, but when it came to his unjust arrest and condemnation he was
silent. Similarly Paul sometimes accepted beatings and imprisonment
without comment, but on other occasions invoked his rights as a
Roman citizen, even to the point of appealing to Caesar.

The second reason Christians find the human rights agenda difficult to
manage is that its focus on the individual cuts across the Bible's concern
for the community and, in particular, for its disadvantaged groups. It is
to this that we must give further attention.

Imagine a Bible-believing church which has enjoyed a period of
renewal. The congregation has grown to the point that an extra Sunday
service is being considered. The homegroups are well attended with
members keen to study the Bible and pray. But progress seems to
have stalled recently, so much so that the leaders have introduced fast
days. Nothing seems able to reverse the sense of decline. So a special

preacher is invited and to the stunned bewilderment of all he lashes the congregation for their sins, even though he acknowledges their enthusiasm and their prayerfulness. Now turn to Isaiah 58 and read a real-life example of such a situation.

What Isaiah describes is a nation which seems bent on pleasing God by doing all the right religious things. The evidence is that they loved God. Then why the prophet's hot breath: 'Declare to my people their rebellion and to the house of Jacob their sins'? You can almost feel the sense of shock rippling through the Temple at his words. The issue was that their love for God was not matched by their love for their neighbour. They had failed to share food with the hungry, justice with the oppressed, shelter for the traveller, clothing with the naked. If only they would do so then the blessings they would enjoy would far exceed anything they had envisaged. It is a matchless picture of the duty and blessing of justice, God's justice expressed through his obedient people. This carries over into the New Testament and the teaching of Jesus.

> Hearing that Jesus had silenced the Sadducees, the Pharisees got together. One of them, an expert in the law, tested him with this question: 'Teacher, which is the greatest commandment in the Law?' Jesus replied: '"Love the Lord your God with all your heart and with all your soul and with all your mind." This is the first and greatest commandment. And the second is like it: "Love your neighbour as yourself." All the Law and the Prophets hang on these two commandments.' (Matt 22:34-40)

Notice that last statement, and particularly the word, 'hang'. It is a carpenter's term for a door hinge - we talk of 'hanging a door'. That's the idea here: all the law turns on these two requirements: love for God and love for neighbour. We need to understand why this is.

JUSTICE AND LOVE

Love is not what we associate most readily with justice. We think more readily of law, of its demands, of its observance, and of retribution in the event of failure to obey it. The Bible speaks of divine justice bringing punishment for wrong,

> The many passages which speak of God's love of justice are not pointing to God's delight over the suffering of those who are justly punished. God's love for justice is grounded in God's love for the victims of injustice - for those who are morally violated.[2]

God's love of justice is mentioned many times in Scripture. Here are some examples:

> For the Lord is righteous, he loves justice.   (Ps 11:7)
>
> The Lord loves righteousness and justice.   (Ps 33:5)
>
> The King is mighty, he loves justice.   (Ps 99:4)
>
> I am the Lord, who exercises kindness, justice and righteousness on earth, for in these I delight. (Jer 9:24)

God is repeatedly said to exercise justice himself and, typically, it is for those who are in need: people who are poor or oppressed, widows, aliens, orphans. There are scores of references of which only a small sample is needed here to make the point:

> The Lord works righteousness and justice for all the oppressed. (Ps 103:6)
>
> I know that the Lord secures justice for the poor and upholds the cause of the needy. (Ps 140:12)

> He upholds the cause of the oppressed and gives food to the hungry. The Lord sets prisoners free, the Lord gives sight to the blind, the Lord lifts up those who are bowed down, the Lord loves the righteous. The Lord watches over the alien and sustains the fatherless and the widow. (Ps 146:7-9)

> Stop doing wrong, learn to do right! Seek justice, encourage the oppressed. Defend the cause of the fatherless, plead the case of the widow.' (Isa 1:17)

The prophets have much to say about the failure of God's people to fulfil the law in respect of the poor. As we have seen above, Isaiah spoke out God's penetrating judgement of Israel's sinful neglect of those for whom God was concerned. Amos is blistering in the bluntness of his condemnation of the selfishness and greed which would bring God's punishment. (Amos 2:6,7). Zechariah too spoke out what God gave him to say:

> This is what the Lord Almighty says, 'Administer true justice; show mercy and compassion to one another. Do not oppress the widow or the fatherless, the alien or the poor.' (Zech 7:8-10)

Jeremiah goes further, suggesting that justice is of the essence of knowing God:

> 'He defended the cause of the poor and needy, so all went well. Is that not what it means to know me?' declares the Lord. (Jer 22:16)

> To become just, a society must bring into community all its weak defenceless ones, its marginal ones, giving them voice and a fair share in the goods of the community.[3]

No mention is made of the circumstances which led to people being socially and economically deprived. The economic structures of society were such that self-sufficiency depended on inherited land, and those who had no such inheritance, for whatever reason, were seriously disadvantaged. Widows were dependant on male relatives for support, as were orphans. Immigrants, the aliens who are frequently mentioned in the Old Testament, would have to find a market for their skills if they were to get by, but if that proved impossible the community was expected to accept and nurture them.

Again and again God reminds his people that the just love they are to show to others is a mirror of what they received from him. The deliverance of Israel from Egypt is repeatedly used as the yardstick for the compassion they in turn are duty bound to express. In his farewell sermon Moses was at pains to make the point more than once:

> For the Lord your God is God of gods and Lord of lords, the great God, mighty and awesome, who shows no partiality and accepts no bribes. He defends the cause of the fatherless and the widow, and loves the alien, giving him food and clothing. And you are to love those who are aliens, for you yourselves were aliens in Egypt. (Dt 10:17-19)

> Do not deprive the alien or the fatherless of justice, or take the cloak of the widow as pledge. Remember that you were slaves in Egypt and the Lord your God redeemed you from there. That is why I command you to do this. (Dt 24:17,18)

In such expressions of justice the Israelites would at the same time be achieving more than simply aiding another person.

> The requirement to do justice is rooted in the requirement to respect the image of God in persons; honouring that image requires honouring the legitimate claims of that person.[4]

So once again the fact that we are made in God's image is invoked to shape our actions, this time not because it points to the value of the person needing our help but in order that through our behaviour people might better understand the justice of God expressed in loving action towards others.

JUSTICE AND HOLINESS

Just as Christians are required to be living expressions of God's love (see Ch 3) so too they are called to be God-like in holiness: 'It is written: "Be holy, because I am holy"'. (1 Pet 1:16)

Just as God-like love is practical so too is God-like holiness. Practical holiness finds expression particularly in respect of justice.

It will already be obvious from the verses quoted above that justice and righteousness are frequently paired in the Old Testament. It is not necessary to decide which is most important as they are almost indivisible.

> The same word in the original becomes in English 'justice' or 'righteousness', almost, one would suspect, at the whim of the translator.[5]
>
> A W TOZER

This helps to explain an apparent inconsistency in Scripture - that this is an Old Testament issue of no relevance to the New Testament. You will have noticed that all the Scriptures so far quoted concerning justice are drawn from the Old Testament. Translators of the New Testament have generally preferred to use 'righteousness' rather than 'justice' but in most instances the terms are interchangeable. Try it; you will find some interesting new perspectives.

Should we then abandon the two terms and settle for the better understood 'justice'? No, because although they mean the same we are able to shade in differences of emphasis between them. Justice focuses on ensuring that right is done and seen to be done. Righteousness brings out the spirit in which right is done. It designates loyalty to a family relationship and behaviour appropriate to that relationship - in short the covenantal family that we are in Christ. And it takes us back yet again to the concept of being made in the image of God.

> Righteousness entails the acceptance of one's identity as the image of God and the consequent obligation of service . . . Righteousness has both a personal and ethical dimension: it is love of family members, accompanied by conformity to a set of house rules which govern the everyday life of the family.[6]

It is now easier to see how justice and holiness relate to one another. They are bound together in the response required to vulnerable people. In the story of Israel people who are advantaged and disadvantaged, rich and poor, able and disabled are part of the same family. They were bound together by the same covenantal relationship and subject to exactly the same commandments and laws. To be holy or righteous was also to be just towards all.

The same theme, predictably, applies in the New Testament in respect of the church. What Paul has to say about righteousness follows the same broad outlines we see in the Old Testament.

> Righteousness has primary reference to the way in which Christians relate to one another in the body of Christ, under his Lordship and governed by his law.[7]

Expressions of mutual love within the Christian family are acts of righteousness (justice) and serve to support one another, especially the weak and those who have fallen back into sin. This same righteousness, in turn, permits the Christian to reach out to others as they also bear the image of God.

Justice is something we typically associate with other groups of people - lawyers, judges, politicians - and with other places - law courts and parliaments. What the Bible brings home to us has far more to do with the way the Christian behaves and relates to other people. Justice is integral to our being part of the family of God. It is to shape how we live together in the body of Christ and how we express the image of God in us to the world about us. It is inevitable, then, that we will be different and distinctive - or holy. How could we possibly image God and be unholy!

JUSTICE AND PEACE

The Hebrew word for peace is 'shalom'. It is better translated 'flourishing' than 'peace'. It goes beyond the mere absence of hostility to suggest flourishing in all one's relationships - with God, with others, with one's self, and with creation. It is a condition that is only possible where there is justice.

Isaiah envisages a time when this will be fully realised in a world ruled by the King of Righteousness:

> Justice will dwell in the desert and righteousness live in the fertile field. The fruit of righteousness will be peace; the effect of righteousness will be quietness and confidence for ever. My people will live in peaceful dwelling places. (Isa 32:16-18)
>
> Love and faithfulness meet together, righteousness and peace kiss each other. (Ps 85:10)

The contrast with our present experience is stark, but the partial realisation of it is surely possible where Christians give expression to the sort of justice that the Bible commends to us and commands of us.

There is a clear mandate in Scripture for Christians to be engaged in justice, but not solely or simply out of a concern for laws which reflect Biblical values. True justice is something which all believers are called to express in their response to people as well as to issues. Indeed the focus of Scripture is very much on justice as integral to the image of God in us, portraying the God whose image is thus revealed in us and by us.

[1] Os Guinness, *The Call* p90/92

[2] *New Dictionary of Christian Ethics and Pastoral Theology* p18

[3] ibid p18

[4] ibid p18

[5] A W Tozer, *Knowledge of the Holy* p92
For the sake of accuracy the following comment by Wayne Grudem should be noted: 'The English terms righteousness and justice are different words but in both the Hebrew Old Testament and the Greek New Testament there is only one word group behind these two English terms.' Systematic Theology p204

[6] *New Dictionary of Christian Ethics and Pastoral Theology* p744

[7] ibid p744

NB After completing the manuscript for this book I discovered *Generous Justice* by Tim Keller. It looks at this theme far more thoroughly than I have attempted in this chapter and is highly recommended for further study of what the Bible has to say about the relationship between justice and grace.

CHAPTER 5
A DIFFERENT SENSE OF HOPE

THE PLACE OF HOPE

Maybe Karl Marx was not so far out in fact. He was making a serious point when he wrote:

> Religion is the sigh of the oppressed creature, the heart of a heartless world. . . It is the opium of the people.' [1]

He described what he had observed on continental Europe and in his adopted city of London. It was a society of zero social mobility. As you were born so you would die. It was celebrated in C F Alexander's popular hymn, 'All things bright and beautiful . . .' with a verse long since excised from our hymn books:

> The rich man in his castle
>   the poor man at his gate,
> God made them high or lowly
>   and ordered their estate. [2]

It wasn't possible for poor people to change this but if they behaved themselves things would turn out alright in the end: they could hope for heaven. Their potentially revolutionary fervour was stilled, Marx argued, with religion's false bribe.

Similar objections against religion are still being made, even though we have long since left behind the social apartheid of previous centuries. New Atheism is still speaking of religion as repressive, as holding its adherents in thrall to utopian fantasies of life hereafter. Whether we like it or not, that is the religion they see on every hand. If they look at Islam they may see an educated and intelligent young man offering himself as a suicide bomber to gain the status of martyr with its promise of heaven. Short of that, the faithful can only hope that their efforts will suffice to secure them a place in paradise. The Christianity most people see - whether Orthodox, Catholic or Protestant - seems to present a more peaceful version of roughly the same principle: be good, give to charity, add a splash of religion and a benign God will accept you into his heaven if you ask nicely! Such religions may inspire fear or wishful thinking, but they do not inspire much admiration or respect. If that really were all that is on offer, surely humanism would be vastly more popular than it has yet managed to become.

Our concern, however, is not religion as such, but Biblical Christianity, the sort of practical faith-filled spirituality of Jesus. This is no repressive system to anaesthetise us with fantasies. This is a faith which speaks a message vital to an age such as ours where hope is hard to find.

> Hopelessness, anxiety, pessimism, discouragement, dread and despair are epidemic in our era.[3]

Could it be that this is in some way connected to the spread of secularism?

> Hope is a basic human need. We live very much in our hopes
> and invest much of ourselves in them, and it would be soul-
> destroying in the most literal sense to have all hopes taken
> away. We say, 'While there's life, there's hope; equally true,
> and equally basic, is the reverse statement: 'While there's hope,
> there's life'.[4]

J PACKER

Any conversation about hope is dogged by the different ways in
which the word is used. In the vocabulary of everyday it includes
dreams, fantasies, wishes - all with, or without, any realistic possibility
of fulfilment. We drive off for our day on the beach in spite of the
gathering clouds. The under-qualified student applies for a course for
which his grades are insufficient. The love-struck man sends yet another
optimistic Valentine's bouquet - and so on. In the language of Scripture
'hope' has an altogether different strength. It rings with certainty,
confidence, predictability. Hope has been described as 'the future tense
of faith'. Like faith and love it is of the essence of Christian experience.

When this study was first planned I was inclined to omit hope as a
motivation for responding to human need. Knowing humanism's jibe
that we only do religion to get 'pie in the sky when we die', it seemed
sensible to sidestep the issue. But why should we be embarrassed to
speak this encouraging and important truth because of the ignorance
of others? If we are motivated at all to show God's love to others, let it
be in the full enjoyment of all the good that may flow from what we do
- here AND hereafter!

THE BASIS OF HOPE

We know that this life is but one phase of the existence we have been
given. There is within us the strong sense that this is not all and it is
not everything.

> For, whatever we say to the contrary (and bravado leads many modern sophisticates to claim the contrary), we cannot stop hoping that there is something more to life than the merely physical, and we cannot stop hoping that meaningful personal survival is included in that 'something more'.[5]
>
> J PACKER

The atheist urges us to enjoy the now as much as we can because it is all we are going to get. The Bible tells us that God has indeed given us this world to be 'richly enjoyed' - and there is more and better to come! Whether we get the opportunity to enjoy the 'better to come' will depend on what has happened - and on what happens - in the here and now.

The Bible is very clear in what it says about how a person's eternal future is secured. The fact that it has been scandalously misrepresented both by the Church and its opponents is a matter of regret; the results have been disastrous for many. Many will say that our future depends on what we do: Scripture tells us that it depends on what has been done. The forgiveness of sins which we so desperately need has been secured by the death of Christ on the cross.

> Praise be to the God and Father of our Lord Jesus Christ! In his great mercy he has given us new birth into a living hope through the resurrection of Jesus Christ from the dead . . . Through him you believe in God, who raised him from the dead and glorified him, and so your faith and hope are in God. (1 Pet 1 : 3, 21)

It couldn't be much clearer than that! So the eternal life of which the Bible speaks can be known now and is guaranteed by the historical fact that Jesus rose from death and lives for us in heaven.

> If there is no resurrection from the dead, then not even Christ has been raised. And if Christ has not been raised, our preaching

is useless and so is your faith. . . If only for this life we have hope in Christ, we are to be pitied more than all men. But Christ has indeed been raised . . . (1 Cor 15:13,14,19)

A RELATIONAL HOPE

You may have noticed already that relationships form a sub-theme through this study. Reference has been made many times to relationships with God, with one another, with ourselves, and with God's world. That theme bursts into a new dimension when we consider Christian hope.

> ['Faith', 'love', and 'hope'] as Christians use them, all point beyond themselves. They denote relational realities which in each case spring from God himself and return to him. They signify, in other words, a precise relationship to God based on what God himself has revealed. Christian hope arises in response to what God has told us about himself. Like every other detail of the Gospel, it is focused on Jesus Christ. 'He is our hope', affirms the New Testament (1 Tim 1:1) . . . because in him all the promises of God find their fulfilment. (2 Cor 1:20)[6]
>
> J PACKER

Heaven is not about harp-twanging or cloud-floating. It is about realising to the full the relationship we have with God the Father, God the Son and God the Holy Spirit, which began the moment we first trusted in Christ. It is a perennial puzzle why people who have spent their lives without a thought of God, or worse, opposing him, should want to spend eternity in his company. Surely that would be a sort of hell! It is those who know him now, who have some insight from their reading of Scripture and from their personal encounters of God in prayer and everyday experience, who will look forward eagerly to seeing him face to face. The hints of his loveliness, the pointers to his grace, the indications of his goodness whet our appetites for more.

HOPE'S PROSPECT

We human beings are accountable. We don't need to be told this; we feel it within ourselves. But this sense of accountability is not just about what is seen by our peers, or the society in which we live. Much of what we do and who we are is within us, thankfully unseen by others; but even so we sense that Someone is watching us. It is not a divine device to intimidate us nor is it a religious ruse to keep us in our place. It is a recognition of our dignity as persons that we, and we only in the whole of creation, know that we are responsible for our conduct. What is more this fact reassures that there will be true justice in the overall scheme of things.

The first thing to note is that we are given clear warning of what is to happen.

> We must all appear before the judgement seat of Christ, that each one may receive what is due to him for the things done while in the body, whether good or bad. (2 Cor 5:10)

It is right and just that we should be alerted to this fact so we find the theme recurring in various forms through Scripture, from Moses to Malachi, from the prophets to Paul, and supremely from Jesus himself.

The second thing to note is that the Bible nowhere suggests that the Judgement Day will decide whether or not we will be admitted to heaven. Our condemnation or salvation does not depend on how well we have kept the rules or 'done the right thing'.

> Whoever believes in him [Jesus] is not condemned, but whoever does not believe is condemned already because he has not believed in the name of God's one and only Son'. (John 3:18)

Salvation from sin is far more serious and costly than could be bought by the occasional deed of kindness or church attendance. It cost the life of the Son of God and it is obtained only when we put our faith in him.

> When the kindness and love of God our Saviour appeared, he
> saved us, not because of righteous things we had done, but
> because of his mercy.
> (Tit 3:4,5)

Which brings us to a third issue of note: those who know their sins
are forgiven will want to live gratefully by serving their Saviour. He
encourages us in this by promising that he will reward our efforts.
At this point some believers may feel uncomfortable with the idea of
working for and looking forward to rewards. It feels so mercenary!
Shouldn't we do good for its own sake? Nothing, however, is quite
that simple. Working for rewards is already part of the warp and woof
of our lives. We go to work in the expectation of being rewarded at the
end of week or month. (We may feel that we are worth a good deal
more than the reward we will receive, but we still turn up on Monday
morning.) But few of us would find the wage a sufficient reward if
we did not find our work in some way and to some degree fulfilling
or enjoyable. There will be other motivations to get us to our work-
place: we want to keep a roof over our head, feed our family, clothe
our children, and so on. It is much the same with the prospect of future
rewards for our Christian service: there are many more reasons for
doing good than hoping for a crown!

On the night he was betrayed Jesus told his disciples, 'If you love me,
you will obey what I command'. (Jn 14:15) Of course they would. We
hardly need to be urged to do our very best for someone we love. It
is done willingly, enthusiastically so as to bring pleasure to the loved
one - which in itself is rewarding. In the same way Christian service
is relational. It is because I love God that I want to do what he wants
me to do so as to please and honour him. Is it any wonder that this is
so? God has shown astonishing commitment to us as Christians. The
story of the prodigal son (Lk 15:11-20) shows how God the Father
longed for us to come to him. The story of the lost sheep (Lk 15:1-7)

shows how God the Son, the Good Shepherd, came looking for us in our lostness. The gift of the Holy Spirit to be with us so that we have strength and grace to live for God further demonstrates that our triune God is utterly devoted to us. How often we have been enriched and blessed beyond our wildest dreams. In many a dark place we have been given light; at times of despair we have been given help and hope; on many a good day we have drunk deeply of unearthly joy. Grateful? Of course we are grateful! And, yes, I will gladly serve my Saviour knowing that, over and above all the blessings I receive here, there are more to come. This is not my primary motivation by any means, but why should it not be something I anticipate with pleasure and hope?

Of course we are not very sure just what the rewards will be. What are the chances that we will be disappointed? The disciples asked Jesus to teach them about prayer and in doing so he posed this question:

> Which of you fathers, if your son asks for a fish, will give him a snake instead?' (Lk11:11)

No answer was called for as it is obvious that a father will do his best to meet his child's request. Just as a child trusts its father so the believer can trust his Saviour. The promises God has made are dependable. And as for the uncertainty as to what the rewards will be, well perhaps they just can't be expressed in our terms. Paul quoted from Isaiah to make the point:

> No eye has seen, no ear has heard, no mind has conceived what God has prepared for those who love him. (1 Cor 2:9)

We are unable adequately to describe the eternal realm because all our categories would be understatements of its wonders. All our analogies are as incomplete as seeds are to describe the fruits and flowers they hide within their dull shell. What we know and see here is but a shadow of what will be. It is a form of existence for which we have no vocabulary. Every Biblical picture stretches our language and concept to breaking point in an attempt to describe the beauty, wonder and joy of eternity and heaven.

Can we discover nothing, then, about the rewards which await those who serve their Saviour? There are two things we can say from Scripture: the first is that rewards will be proportional to service. God has a purpose for us, a role for us to fulfil; our salvation was intentional.

> For we are God's workmanship, created in Christ Jesus to do good works, which God has prepared in advance for us to do. (Eph 2:10)

Paul elsewhere uses an analogy from building to express both elements of this - what God has done for us and what we are called to do for God.

> For no one can lay any foundation other than the one already laid, which is Jesus Christ. If any man builds on this foundation using gold, costly stones, wood, hay or straw, his work will be shown for what it is because the Day will bring it to light. It will be revealed with fire, and the fire will test the quality of each man's work. If what he has built survives, he will receive his reward. If it is burned up, he will suffer loss; he himself will be saved, but only as one escaping through the flames. (1Cor 3:11-15)

Graphic but graspable! The same principle is evident in the parable of the talents told by Jesus. (Mt 25:14-30)

Secondly, Christian service and its rewards are seen in very personal terms. What we do may benefit a variety of people and situations but Jesus regards it as something done to and for him. Another long quotation, this time from Jesus himself, shows this clearly:

When the Son of Man comes in his glory, and all the angels with him, he will sit on his glorious throne. All the nations will be gathered before him, and he will separate the people one from another as a shepherd separates the sheep from the goats. He will put the sheep on his right and the goats on his left.

Then the King will say to those on his right, 'Come, you who are blessed by my Father; take your inheritance, the kingdom prepared for you since the creation of the world. For I was hungry and you gave me something to eat, I was thirsty and you gave me something to drink, I was a stranger and you invited me in, I needed clothes and you clothed me, I was sick and you looked after me, I was in prison and you came to visit me.'

Then the righteous will answer him, 'Lord, when did we see you hungry and feed you, or thirsty and give you something to drink? When did we see you a stranger and invite you in, or needing clothes and clothe you? When did we see you sick or in prison and go to visit you?'

The King will reply, 'Truly I tell you, whatever you did for one of the least of these brothers of mine, you did for me.'
(Mt 25:31-40)

He goes on to say the converse to 'the goats' on his left hand. Far from being a confirmation that we earn our acceptance with God Jesus clearly states the opposite. The first act of the King in the parable is to separate sheep from goats - ie the saved from the unsaved. The works he commends are the outcome and expression of that salvation. Saved to do good, which is what the rest of the New Testament affirms.

Humanism promotes a very different sort of hope that is entirely temporal (of course) and far less certain.

> One major hope for the future is science . . . When science
> replaces mythology [code word for religion, particularly
> Christianity] as the framework for understanding the world,
> it brings with it its enquiring, questioning, open-minded
> attitudes, and that in turn . . . makes possible a better and finer
> understanding of what conduces to the human good.[7]
>
> A C GRAYLING

It is hopeful but perhaps rather wishful thinking given that centuries
of science and millennia of philosophy have yet to discover such basic
human needs. We do not have time to wait for further centuries to
pass for 'the human good' to spring from the test tube of science or
the silicone chip of a computer. Nor do we need to wait when the
strong hope revealed in Scripture has proved real in our experience
and motivates us to a compassionate and rewarding response to those
in need.

[1] Quoted by A McGrath in *The Twilight of Atheism* p66

[2] Quoted from memory - I hope accurately!

[3] *The New Dictionary of Christian Ethics and Pastoral Theology* p457

[4] James Packer and Thomas Howard, *Christianity: the True Humanism* p80

[5] ibid p84

[6] ibid p92/3

[7] A C Grayling, *What is Good?* p 243/6 (parenthesis mine)

CHAPTER 6
THE WORLD AHEAD OF US

Futurology seems to me more of a sport than a science, a game of aiming at targets, sometimes hitting, sometimes missing. Back in the late 1960s Alvin Toffler wrote a popular book entitled simply, *Futurology*. He followed it with another in the 1970s, and still another subsequently. They were all fascinating attempts to predict trends for the coming years. Some of his predictions came true, like the expectation that every home would have its own computer, a seemingly improbable idea in the days before Windows. He was right of course, except that he said it would happen by at least 1980, whereas it was the turn of the century before it was anything like realised.

However well we know the past and the present, the future is unknowable, but not entirely so. We can safely expect many of today's trends to continue into the future. Attitudes and beliefs change only slowly, so although ten years from now they may be quite different, tomorrow's society will look and feel and think much as it does today. We can fairly safely assume that the creeping spread of secularism will advance further. Even where churches see some growth and progress the proportion of people indifferent to or ignorant of the gospel in the United Kingdom - assuming that it will still be united! - will steadily increase. Unless of course there is a revival, then things will change rapidly and beneficially. That, however, is unpredictable. God chooses to keep his plans secret on the matter. Apart from such a supernatural intervention we who serve God will do so in the context of unbelief.

There will be opportunities to do good as individual Christians - and that we must do. There is also need to do good as Christians working together to give expression to the values we share: so much of what is needed cannot be achieved without our helping one another. The existence of numerous Christian organisations and charities is testament to that fact and to the strength of a Christian response to the breadth of need. They represent a wide range of issues: from helping people deal with debt to helping tax-efficient giving to charity; from supporting people with disabilities to feeding people who are homeless; from evangelising children to evangelising Chad. Whether long-term or short-term intervention, whether for old people or young people, whether church planting or church building, whether lobbying politicians or Church leaders, wherever Christians see the need for compassion or conviction they are there. This sort of commitment has changed individuals, families and communities down through the centuries. There is no reason for it to stop now or in the foreseeable future, just as there is no reason for it to be absorbed into the secularism of our age. Leo Tolstoy observed:

> Science gives no answer to the only question important to us: 'What shall we do and how shall we live?'[1]

> It's obvious when you think about it: that's not what science is for! 'True science is always provisional . . . In true science the latest word is never the last word.'[2]

> J BLANCHARD

It should therefore be no surprise that Christianity, founded as it is on God's revelation, differs substantially from a humanism preoccupied with being 'scientific'. Nor should it surprise us when we find that we are striking out in a different and distinctive direction to tackle the mountainous problems which confront us in the world.

Given what we have seen in this study we must now face the question, 'How?' How do we give expression to this distinctive teaching of Scripture? How are our Christian lives and organisations to work these principles into the practical activities which engage us? If a different sense of value, of freedom, of justice and of hope are to be on display, what does that mean in our everyday lives and work?

Secularism trumpets two key words to convey its message: freedom and autonomy. The Christian response is in one key word: love. Not the sentimental and romantic emotion of literature, film and ballad but the strong, practical concern and compassion which God has for our broken world. And if we need another word for 'love in practice' then the Bible provides us with one: service. Over against the individualism of the age the Bible calls us to a less self-obsessed concern for others and for the community around us. At the same time this unselfish love and service flows from a relationship: our relationship with the Lord Jesus Christ. He is the inspiration we need, his the example we follow and his Spirit the strength we receive.

MANDATE

We are commanded to love and, in the light of what we have discovered about human nature, it makes sense that we should be expected to do so. John declares, 'God is love'. (1 Jn 4:16) Those who image God should be a demonstration of that fact. This love is distinctively Christian. While the New Testament writers made some use the popular Greek word for love 'philia' and they took up the less used 'agape' filling it with new meaning. Philia is the word used for loyalty to friends, family and community. It is warm with feeling, instinctive sentiment and affection. Agape is more about action towards others, wanting the best for them, recognising their value as people. This is love of the will rather than the feelings. This helps us better to understand the way Jesus lived; we see these qualities in the way he related to people.

As we approach the climactic chapters of the Gospels we sense a growing urgency in what Jesus said to his disciples, as if he still had a lot to share with them and little time left to do so. We also see a greater emphasis on some themes, as if he must ensure they have 'got the message'. Two such themes are closely intertwined: love and service. Right through his ministry Jesus had shown and encouraged servant attitudes. To the ambitious James and John he said, 'Whoever wants to become great among you must be your servant,' adding as if to drive the point home, 'For the Son of Man did not come to be served but to serve. . . .' (Mk 10:43,45) Neither they nor the other disciples seem to have grasped the importance of this. On the very eve of the crucifixion, shockingly, the disciples were still arguing about their pecking order - can you believe it! Did the foot-washing precede or follow this argument, I wonder. Jesus told them, 'I am among you as one who serves'. (Lk 22:27) He also gave them a demonstration.

As Jesus prayed later that evening he told his Father that he was replicating his own mission: 'As you sent me into the world, I have sent them into the world.' (Jn 17:18) The Son of God had humbled himself to become a man, and then further to become a servant so as to fulfil his commission. (Phil 2:7) God's purpose for his Son has become God's purpose for us as well: servanthood. It takes love to be this sort of servant.

The New Testament returns to these themes of love and service again and again. The great apostle Paul repeatedly described himself as a servant of Jesus Christ and a servant of the churches. (eg 1 Cor 3:5, 2 Cor 4:5) Instructions on serving Christ, others in the Christian family and those outside of it are reiterated several times. They are seen as the natural and proper expression of Christian living. 'Live as servants of God'. (1 Pet 2:16)

> Christian love belongs rather to the sphere of action than of emotion. It is not an involuntary passion but unselfish service undertaken by deliberate choice. [3]
>
> J STOTT

The mandate is love.

MOTIVATION

Christians recognise that they are to keep God's law and, in intent at least, do so willingly.

> God's commands are no more burdensome than wings are to a bird. They are the means by which we live in freedom and fulfilment. [4]
>
> D JACKMAN

> Freedom is not so much the absence of restrictions as finding the right ones. [5]
>
> T KELLER

> True freedom is not the liberty to do anything we please, but the liberty to do what we ought; and it is genuine liberty because doing what we ought now pleases us. [6]
>
> D A CARSON

Being given laws to direct and govern the way we live is a recognition of the dignity of human beings who alone are given such insights. Living by our Maker's instructions will surely result in the greatest possible fulfilment.

It is not often these days that I find myself reaching for the King James Version of the Bible. I find more modern translations easier to follow and apply. But just occasionally a phrase or verse learned way back comes to mind and seems to capture something missing in later renderings. The KJV renders Psalm 40:8 thus, 'I delight to do thy will, O my God: yea thy law is within my heart.' The NIV renders it, 'I desire to do thy will, O my God.' It has lost the note of enjoyment, of real pleasure to be found in doing what God requires. And there is indeed pleasure to be found in obedience.

Our modern approach to pleasure shines out in the travel pages of the weekend supplements in our newspapers, the holiday adverts on TV - that image of sitting back soaking up the sun in a luxurious setting with waiters hovering to supply our every whim! It casts its spell on us as we toil in the real world of daily work, family responsibilities, legal obligations. By contrast to the dream-like pictures, we discover that doing right not only is good but feels good too. There is fulfilment in seeing the relief in the face of someone who was desperately lonely until you dropped in for a five minute chat. There is delight in sending a gift to feed a hungry child or dig a well in a distant drought ridden village. There is pleasure to be had in knowing that you have done something that brought hope and joy to another human being. There is pleasure to be had too in knowing that God has been pleased by your cooperation and obedience.

The motivation is love.

MANNER

In recent years there has been a series of reports about the care of older people. All the right things were said in response to the issues they raised but nothing much changed. A commission was set up by the Local Government Association, the NHS Confederation and Age UK. The preliminary report was published in February 2012 entitled, 'Delivering Dignity: Securing Dignity for Older People in Hospital and Care Homes' It was not altogether pleasant reading. A key recommendation was that appointing staff to care for older people should ensure that they are first and foremost caring and compassionate people. This, it said, was more important than the skills they possess! (Did we need a high level report to tell us this?) It implied a disturbing lack of compassion as the key problem in existing staff and services.

In 2011 a BBC Panorama programme reported on a 'hospital' for people with learning disabilities who also present challenging behaviours. We watched in horror secretly filmed abuse perpetrated by staff of Winterbourne View Hospital. It brought condemnation from the Prime Minister, the closure of the hospital and the subsequent trial and punishment of staff responsible for the atrocities.

What is it that goads people to behave as they do in these circumstances? Perhaps it is power. The social and health care services are extraordinarily structured, with layer upon layer of power. These layers structure the local unit and on to district, regional and national levels, taking in commissioners and regulators, quangos and government departments, until the voice of the individual in need has long since been 'tuned out' in the welter of checklists, assessments, policies and eventual legislation. Meanwhile, who will hear the frail, elderly Mrs Smith feebly calling for someone to help her reach the meal left on her hospital table? Who will notice John struggling to overcome his learning disability to describe his hopes for today? Power is anti-gravitational - unlike water it only runs uphill, leaving those 'at the bottom' weaker and more vulnerable than ever. Which is why the report, 'Delivering Dignity', emphasised the point in respect of elderly people:

> There is an imbalance of power in the relationship between a person receiving care and the staff delivering it. Those staff who provide dignified care constantly seek to redress this imbalance by involving the individual in decisions wherever possible, explaining what is happening and why, listening to and addressing concerns, and above all treating each person as someone deserving respect, understanding, empathy and kindness. In short they recognise care as a partnership instead of treating older people as passive recipients.[7]

Christians may feel these pressures as much as anyone else. Working with dependent people can be incredibly demanding and draining. With limited time it is far quicker to do things for people, to make decisions for them, rather than waiting and listening and responding to their wishes. Supporting people who have become incorrigibly unreasonable, demanding, awkward and difficult requires the patience (and love) of a saint if one is not to lose patience or temper or both. And this is just what we Christians are called to be - saints, those who serve others. The advantage of being one who is called is that the One who calls us provides the resources with which to fulfil the calling. Paul calls it 'the fruit of the Spirit'. It is precisely what is needed if we are to express the distinctive life of Christ in the work we engage in.

> The fruit of the Spirit is love, joy, peace, patience, kindness, goodness, faithfulness, gentleness and self-control. (Gal 5:22)

Like all fruit, this does not appear fully formed the day after conversion but gradually as we draw on the Spirit's life to serve our Saviour.

Imagine the powerful effect of this fruit - it is singular, a fruit, by the way, not plural - on a distressed person with a learning disability, on a disoriented old man or woman with Alzheimer's disease, on a disaffected youngster. A gentler, kinder, stronger, cheerful person alongside patiently supporting and encouraging someone who is angry or afraid or confused or misunderstood - what a shaft of light in a potentially dark place, where otherwise there might be noise, control, the threat of punishment.

Imagine how much more convincing an argument delivered with courtesy to a parliamentarian or local councillor or police officer can be than a banner-waving harangue. How much more effective practical advice to a harassed single mother or a debt-laden husband than finger-pointing condemnation.

The Gospel tells us both what to do and how to do it, method and manner. Jesus was noted for what he said and the way he said: 'gracious words'.

The manner is love.

The world ahead of us may turn out to be very different from the one we are already leaving behind. There is no reason to believe that it will leave us marooned on a tiny island called 'Religion', much as the humanist lobby might wish it. There is still a role for us to serve God in the world by responding to the challenges and needs that society presents. We may need to be more adaptable, more flexible, more innovative as those needs and opportunities change. We may have to make greater sacrifices as funding sources are constrained or closed off. But of this we can be sure: Christian love will still find ways to serve.

Christianity is, after all, as James Packer rightly claimed, 'the true humanism'. It is not reason that makes us human.

> What makes us human is not our mind but our heart, not our ability to think but our ability to love.[8]
>
> H M NOUWEN

Which is what is so distinctive about the greatest, truest human being who ever lived: the Lord Jesus Christ.

LOVE IS THE REASON.

[1] Quoted by Os Guinness, *The Call* p4

[2] John Blanchard, *Does God believe in Atheists*, p431

[3] John Stott, *Tyndale New Testament Commentary on the Letters of John*, p207

[4] David Jackman, *The Message of John's Letters*, p141

[5] T Keller, *The Reason for God*, p146

[6] D A Carson quoted by B Milne in *The Message of John*, p134

[7] *Delivering Dignity*, Commission on Dignity in Care for Older People, p12

[8] H M Nouwen quoted by Philip Yancey in *Soul Survivor*, p296

APPENDIX A AIDE MEMOIRE

The intention of this appendix is to provide a summary of the arguments of the book as an aid to memory when Christians face situations where their practice or their right to practice is subject to challenge, or to facilitate discussions with government agencies or grant-making bodies. The arguments and principles of the book are set out more fully in the chapters which precede this section.

CHAPTER 1 THE WORLD ABOUT US

How should Christians respond to the troubles faced by society, especially in times of austerity?

THE SOLUTION OF SECULARISM

Society has become substantially influenced by humanism. Our culture is dominated by belief in the freedom and autonomy of the individual as of primary importance. Discussion of moral issues is now conducted on this basis rather than on generally agreed principles. Science has become the authority on how we perceive ourselves and our world. Religion is a problem and should be restricted to the sphere of private and personal belief.

THE CHRISTIAN RESPONSE

The Bible expects Christians to be different from the rest of society. They belong to God's Kingdom and God's community as well as their own networks and communities. They also belong to the Body of Christ. This results in Christian motivation, values, freedom, justice and hope. Our religion is incomplete if it is only a matter of private belief; it requires us to engage with the world about us.

CHAPTER 2 A DIFFERENT SENSE OF VALUE

It may help to remember the headings of this chapter if you notice that the first letters make the word GIVE.

GOD - PRIORITY

Secularism does not understand that Christians are people who have a relationship with God, who know God. It imagines that we are cowed into observing religious rules by our fear of a hostile deity or of final condemnation. Knowing God is both real, reasonable and rooted in history. This reality has priority over every sphere of the Christian's life.

IMAGE - PERSONHOOD

'What is man?' This is the major moral and ethical question of the day. The answer must include every human being and every aspect of human-ness. The Bible provides the answer in its opening chapter:

> Then God said, 'Let us make man in our image, in our likeness . . .' So God created man in his own image, in the image of God he created him; male and female he created them. (Gen 1:26,27)

Human beings are uniquely made in the image of God and, although that image was damaged by our fall into sin, it remains as the distinguishing mark of what it means to be human. God-likeness is evident in a capacity for relationships, in spirituality, in moral awareness, in rational thought, in creativity, in humour, and more.

VALUE - PRECIOUS

Secularism struggles with the concept of human worth. We feel that we are precious and significant, but what is it that gives us this sense of value? The Bible's answer is that our value lies in the fact that we are bear the image of God. This fact made the incarnation possible and the cross inevitable to the God whose image we bear.

This concept of the value of every individual results in a positive welcoming of the diversity we find among human beings. It has the power to restore a sense of dignity to people of all sorts, at every level of society. Everyone is to be valued.

EXPECTATION - POTENTIAL

The life of Jesus shows us what God's image in a human being can be like. Being God he fulfilled all the potential of the image of God in a human being. The New Testament teaches that someone who believes in Christ can be changed to become increasingly like him. This opens up wonderful possibilities for us, and for others.

CHAPTER 3 A DIFFERENT SENSE OF FREEDOM

Humanism makes freedom its priority - by which it means freedom from an externally imposed morality. But, as in nature, so in the rest of life our freedoms are subject to laws and constraints. Society needs a moral framework. Discovering the humanist framework is difficult as each writer seems to follow a different route. Humanism generally promotes the view that right actions are those which promote the greatest pleasure for those affected.

The Bible's approach to morality sets boundaries within which freedom takes the form of beneficial and fulfilling activity. It is 'the perfect law that gives freedom'. (James 1:25) The New Testament ideal of 'the good life' is exemplified by Jesus Christ who 'came to serve'. The Christian is called to a freedom that serves others rather than self-interest. The 'rule' for Christian freedom is love.

CHAPTER 4 A DIFFERENT SENSE OF JUSTICE

Christians are uncomfortable with a view of justice primarily based on human rights because of its focus on one's own concerns. It sees justice in terms of love for one's neighbour, and in particular, people who are disadvantaged and vulnerable.

JUSTICE AND LOVE

God's love of justice is grounded in his love for the victims of injustice. Israel's past experience of injustice was expected to teach them compassion for those who suffered it. Respect for the image of God in people requires honouring their rightful claims.

JUSTICE AND HOLINESS

Justice and righteousness are two sides of the same coin: one expressing what is to be done, the other expressing the spirit in which it is done. It has reference to the way Christians behave and relate to other people.

JUSTICE AND PEACE

True justice is concerned for the well-being of others, not merely the fulfilment of legislation. Its expression is integral to the image of God in us.

CHAPTER 5 A DIFFERENT SENSE OF HOPE

THE PLACE OF HOPE

Biblical Christianity addresses the fundamental human need of hope, of certainty in the face of an uncertain future.

THE BASIS OF HOPE

The assurance of eternal life is possible to those who believe in Christ. His resurrection is the guarantee of eternal life for believers.

A RELATIONAL HOPE

Heaven is about being with the God we have come to know through believing in Jesus.

HOPE'S PROSPECT

Human beings will be called to account at the last judgement. This will not determine their final destiny as that is dependent on whether or not we have received by faith the salvation Jesus died to obtain for us. Benefitting from his death, Christians will want to live gratefully.

CHAPTER 6 THE WORLD AHEAD OF US

We can expect that secularism will advance in the future. Christians will be called to serve God in a context increasingly marked by agnosticism and atheism. How the principles we hold are expressed will be very important. The key theme of the Christian's response is love.

MANDATE

We are commanded to love - to express God's love by serving others.

MOTIVATION

Love for God is what motivates our obedience, which in turn results in fulfilment for those who obey. It is their pleasure!

MANNER

Expressing love in compassionate caring service flows from the vitality of the Holy Spirit's presence in the Christian.

APPENDIX B BOOK LIST

Sometimes when reading one comes across a sentence or paragraph which seems to capture a big truth in a few words or cuts through to the heart of an issue. For years now I have kept a notebook of such quotes from books I have read. Leafing through it when writing this study I found far more relating to the themes addressed than could be used - without making it more of an anthology of quotations! The problem with this, however, is that my notebook does not include all the publishing data that would normally be included in referenced quotes.

The other problem is that many of the books to which I refer have long since gone out of print. It may be possible to track some down through Google but, by and large, you will have to trust that I have quoted accurately and in context.

Books read in the process of preparing for and writing this book included:

Alistair McGrath, *The Twilight of Atheism,* Rider, 2004

A A Hoekema, *Created in God's Image,* Eerdmans 1986

James Packer and Thomas Howard, *Christianity, The True Humanism,*
Word 1985

A C Grayling, *What is Good?* Weidenfeld and Nicholson, 2007

Stephen Law, *Humanism: A Very Short Introduction,* Oxford University Press 2011

The Care Quality Commission, *The state of health and adult social care in England* 2011

The Equality and Human Rights Commission, *Hidden in plain sight: inquiry into disability related harassment,* 2011

Anthony Flew and Roy Varghese, *There is a God: How the world's most notorious atheist changed his mind,* Kindle edition, 2009

Miriam Boleyn-Fitzgerald, *Pictures of the Mind: What neuroscience tells us about who we are,* Kindle edition, 2010

LGA, NHS Confederation and Age UK, *Delivering Dignity: Securing dignity in care for older people in hospitals and care homes,* 2012

Paula Clifford, *Theology and International Development* Christian Aid, 2010

Francis Spufford, *Unapologetic: why despite everything Christianity can still make surprising emotional sense,* Faber and Faber, 2012

Douglas Groothuis, *Christian Apologetics,* Inter Varsity Press, 2012

Timothy Keller, *Generous Justice* published by Hodder, 2010

Timothy Keller, *The Reason for God,* Dutton, 2008

John Humphreys, *In God we Doubt,* Hodder, 2007

John Marsh, *Liberal Delusion,* Arena Books, 2012

And, of course, I read Richard Dawkins tirades against religion!

I also used two excellent reference books:

Wayne Grudem, *Systematic Theology,* IVP 1994

The New Dictionary of Christian Ethics and Pastoral Theology, IVP 1995

APPENDIX C   HUMAN RIGHTS

As recently as 25 years ago references to human rights in the media were far, far less than they are today. The 'rights agenda' has become pervasive in political and moral argument, ethical debate, and thus, inevitably, in legislation. So embedded has it become that it is surprising to discover how relatively modern the concept is. The ancient world had nothing quite like it and its advocates struggle to find direct parallels. An English 'Bill of Rights' was passed in the 17th century. In the 18th century both the American Declaration of Independence and the French Declaration of the Rights of Man followed revolution in both those countries.

> Human rights are built on three fundamental principles - dignity, autonomy and human worth. This surely is familiar ground for the Christian. Moreover, the original human rights laws were established in the USA following the remarkable case of Running Bear. He was a native American Indian who objected to the court order that consigned him to live in a reservation. He managed to find representation and the case turned on whether or not he was a human being. If so - he had to accede to the order of the authorities and leave his homeland. If not a human being - he would be allowed to roam free! He lost the case and was compelled to live in a reservation. The principle established has been the foundation of the protection of vulnerable people, including many with disabilities, ever since. The argument is as follows: if everyone has human value we all have a responsibility to recognise this in other people. (Dr P M Oakes Private correspondence)

Modern human rights were, in part at least, a reaction to the atrocities and abuses which took place during the Second World War. The founding of the United Nations in 1945 led in 1948 to the signing by the UN General Assembly of the Universal Declaration of Human Rights. In 1950 the newly formed Council of Europe agreed the European Convention of Human Rights and set up the European Court of Human Rights to ensure its implementation. The terms of the Convention passed into UK law in 1998, overseen by the Equality and Human Rights Commission.

Just what are human rights? They are the rights which every person has by virtue of being human! A UK government website lists them as:

- The right to life
- The right to freedom from torture and degrading treatment
- The right to liberty
- The right to a fair trial
- The right not to be punished for something that wasn't a crime when you did it
- The right to respect for private and family life
- The right to freedom of thought, conscience and religion, and freedom to express your beliefs
- The right to freedom of expression
- The right to freedom of assembly and association
- The right to marry and start a family
- The right not to be discriminated against in respect of these rights and freedoms
- The right to peaceful enjoyment of your property
- The right to an education
- The right to participate in free elections
- The right not to be subjected to the death penalty

For more information see: http://www.direct.gov.uk/en/
governmentcitizensandrights/yourrightsandresponsibilities/
dg_4002951

http://www.equalityhumanrights.com/human-rights/

APPENDIX D   DISABILITY AND THEOLOGY

Let me be frank: I don't 'do' disability theology. I have declined to help when students and academics have asked me to assist in their search for 'a theology of disability'. It reminds me of a friend who set off from Reading to drive to Oxford via the M4. She rang from London asking for directions as she hadn't seen any signs to Oxford along the motorway. There was a simple reason: she had been travelling in the wrong direction. A theology of disability begins at the wrong point and travels in the wrong direction for two reasons.

First it must regard disability as something different and distinct, something other than normal. I'm not at all sure it is as clear as that. There are some people who have conditions which prevent them from functioning in the same way as other people, total blindness for example. But there are many others who have visual impairments which are on a continuum from, say, short-sightedness to complete blindness. At what point does one draw a line which labels one group as disabled? The same continuum can be found in every other form of disability, whether of mind or body. The neat categories to which we can pin descriptive labels may suit local authorities deciding who should have a blue badge but have no place in theology.

Which links with the second reason why seeking a disability theology is misdirected: people with disabilities are, first and foremost, people. Forgive me if that seems obvious, but it is key to understanding and responding to issues surrounding disability. There is no room for thinking in terms of 'us' - ie the able-bodied - and 'them' - the disabled. Today we may be among (more or less!) able-bodied people but tomorrow may be a different story. An accident, an illness or a stroke, and we could each find ourself as much disabled as anyone we know. If we are spared such problems we may find old age itself a disabling condition.

Of course theology has much to say about people with disabilities. It is invaluable in that it provides a reasoned basis for the acceptance of people with disabilities as of equal worth and importance as any other human being. In this, theology stands head and shoulders above humanism which struggles to find a basis for such acceptance - and indeed is sometimes to be heard speaking in discriminatory tones against recognising people with disabilities as of equal standing with the rest of humanity. What follows is a brief exploration of some theological issues which arise in relation to disability in terms of individual spirituality, church life and ministry, and the hope and prospect of ultimate wholeness.

1   DISABILITY AND SALVATION

a.   DISABILITY AND SIN

People are sinners and, as a result, people sin. This uncomfortable fact is clearly taught in the Bible - eg Rom 3:23. Even if we find this offensive we know that it is true. It is evident all around us and, when we are honest, we know it to be true of ourselves. We may not be as bad as some people but we are not as good as we intend to be and are certainly not as good as God expects us to be. We have a significant tendency to self-esteem (aka pride) and self-centredness. We don't want anyone else (least of all God) to tell us what we should or should not do. This is one of the drivers of the opposition of humanism to religion. People with disabilities are no different from the rest of us - they are sinners too. Even when a person is profoundly disabled, carers note the same moral and spiritual strengths and weaknesses as are common to us all.

The question of sin and disability has a particular edge. It was once common for disability to be seen as a judgement for sin on the part of the parents. It was an idea that was even around in the time of Christ. What he said should have settled the matter once and for all.

> As he (Jesus) went along, he saw a man blind from birth. His disciples asked him, 'Rabbi, who sinned, this man or his parents, that he was born blind?' 'Neither this man nor his parents sinned,' said Jesus, 'but this happened that the work of God might be displayed in his life.'(John 9:1-3)

But when I was a boy the same nods and winks and knowing looks passed between neighbours when a family found their child had a disability. Thankfully it is less in evidence in society today, but is still sometimes reflected in attitudes in churches.

The fact that the world is less than perfect is certainly a result of sin. It was sin that resulted in the ground being cursed by God. (Gen 3:17-19) Disability and sickness and floods and earthquakes and the like are among the consequences of the rebellion of our first parents. 'The whole creation is groaning' (Rom 8:22) and longing for the end of the 'present time'. But any suggestion that there is a direct link between one person's disability and their or their parents' sin is ruled out by the words of Jesus.

b.   DISABILITY AND CONVERSION

Everybody needs salvation. If people are to know God and be re-made in the likeness of Christ they need to find forgiveness for sin and be reconciled to God. The Good News declares that salvation has been made possible through the death of Christ on the cross, and it is available to all who turn from their sin and put their faith in the now risen Christ. It is the same for everyone regardless of ability or disability: the same way is open to all and the same salvation is possible for all, from God's perspective.

The same degree of open-ness may not be apparent from the perspective of people with disabilities because the church all too often fails to recognise that the Gospel really is for everyone. This has certainly been the problem facing people with learning disabilities. The assumption has been made that their limited capacity for understanding abstract concepts - like God and sin and faith and forgiveness - is a barrier to their experiencing conversion and becoming Christians. With no theological basis, it is fondly hoped that God will somehow have a 'special' category which will not exclude them. This is a failure both of theology and of understanding of learning disability. Conversion is not primarily about intelligence (read 1 Cor 1:20-25 if you are in any doubt about this). It is about grace and the power of the Spirit in regeneration that is key to conversion. There is no group in the world which should be excluded because of our failure of vision or concern. Of course there are challenges in making truth accessible to people with learning disabilities but the thousands who have found salvation through the ministry of Prospects belie the notion that they can be disregarded.

2   DISABILITY AND CHURCH

If church buildings were indicators of Christian attitudes to people with disabilities then, by and large, they would paint a pretty depressing picture. Those who worship in Victorian and Edwardian buildings recognise that they are anything but welcoming to people with disabilities. Flights of steps to the main entrance give a building an appearance of grandeur (witness St Paul's Cathedral), but present an impassable barrier to someone in a wheelchair or struggling with arthritic knees. The old deacon who excused the lack of a ramp on the grounds wheelchair users didn't come to his church was obviously missing the point!

People with disabilities have often found a less-than-welcoming attitude among Christians. Back in the mid-1980s when a Christian holiday conference began to include sessions for people with learning disabilities in their programme the organisers had such strong reaction that I was interviewed in the main celebration meetings to explain their presence. This reflected a negative outlook which reached back to the Middle Ages, for which an inadequate theology may have been responsible. In an obscure passage in Leviticus (21:16-23) Moses was given instructions which appear to discriminate against people with 'defects' - those who are blind, lame, disfigured, deformed, or with other chronic conditions - barring them from the priesthood. It is important to understand what is - and is not - being said here.

God had set aside one tribe within Israel, the Levites, who would be responsible for the spiritual life of the nation. They were responsible for the Tabernacle, and later the Temple, and for managing the sacrificial systems and worship. During the wilderness wanderings they also undertook all that was involved in dismantling, transporting, re-erecting and protecting the Tabernacle. One family of Levites, Aaron and his direct descendants, were to function as priests. They were to be the intermediaries between God and the people and for this reason the highest standards were to be expected of them. Theirs was the vital role of offering sacrifice on behalf of the nation and of offering the peoples' prayers to God. Effectiveness required that their ministry must be performed free from any defect - ceremonial, moral or physical - in the offerer or the offering. Chapters 21 and 22 of Leviticus set out how that effectiveness could be compromised. Strict observance was required, not because of what it said about the one who made the offering but because of what it declared about the One to whom the offering was made: God himself (Lev 22:31-33). To read these verses as suggesting a negative view of people with disabilities on God's part is to misunderstand their intention (See also Lev 19:14).

The New Testament makes it clear that salvation is like being born into a family, the family of God. Those who become Christians become part of an inclusive community. Another analogy used in the New Testament is that of the Church as the Body of Christ of which every believer is an important part and in which every believer has a function.

> Now the body is not made up of one part but of many. If the foot should say, 'Because I am not a hand, I do not belong to the body,' it would not for that reason cease to be part of the body. . . If the whole body were an eye, where would the sense of hearing be? . . . But in fact God has arranged the parts of the body, every one of them just as he wanted them to be . . . The

head cannot say to the feet, 'I don't need you!' On the contrary, those parts of the body that seem to be weaker are indispensable, and the parts that we think are less honourable we treat with special honour. (1 Cor 12:14-23)

This is not simply 'inclusion' but much more than that: it is recognition that we need one another, regardless of our apparent abilities or spiritual gifts - or lack of them!

There is a further corollary to this in the life of the church: each member must be able to make their distinctive contribution. In the fairly structured life of a local church this tends to be seen in terms of gifts for particular offices: deacon, pastor/teacher, Sunday school teacher, youth worker etc. The assumption may be made that people with disabilities benefit from these roles rather than fulfil them, but this is not necessarily the case. Churches must expect that every person has a contribution to make, regardless of physical or other disability. Hugh's gift was the ability to welcome people as they arrived at church. His smile and warm handshake contributed to the sense of well-being members felt as they arrived. The fact that he had Down's syndrome in no way hindered his effectiveness. A man with cerebral palsy fought for years for the right to be ordained to the ministry to which he felt very strongly called, and eventually won through to become a valued church leader.

Participation in the baptism and communion has also, at times, challenged church attitudes to people with disabilities, particularly those practising believers baptism by immersion. They may restrict one or both to members who can give testimony to conversion, which may prove difficult for a person with a learning disability. For a person in a wheelchair baptism by immersion may be a physical challenge, though I have heard of it happening - wheelchair and all! Surely what the church should identify is evidence of conversion on the basis Jesus gave: 'by their fruits you shall know them'. Beyond that it is down to the church to find ways to make observance of the Lord's commands possible for people with disabilities. Non-Baptists may prove more flexible to their special needs.

If attitudes are right then all the practical considerations for including people of all abilities and disabilities can be addressed. Ramps for access, disabled toilets, clear print in songs projected onto screens, adequate amplification, chairs with arms, specialist ministries - advice and solutions are widely available. These are not so much matters of theology but are critical to its outworking in the life of the church. Thankfully there has been substantial change both in attitudes and facilities in churches. Many groups are actively welcoming and supporting people with disabilities so that they are able to participate as fully as they are able in the life of their local church fellowship.

3 DISABILITY AND ESCHATOLOGY

DISABILITY AND HEALING

Of all the questions raised about disability those about healing are the most common. For many Christians the sight of a wheelchair is a challenge to pray for a miracle. And for many a Christian with a disability the pressure from others to 'believe' for their 'healing' can be immense. Many have left the church disillusioned at the lack of acceptance they felt when the earnest prayers of others did not result in a miracle, as if somehow it was their fault. This is not the place for a full consideration of a complex matter but at least some of the issues need to be faced.

One of the notable elements of the Gospel story is how often Jesus healed people from disabilities: sight was restored to some blind people, hearing to deaf people, speech to a dumb man, the power to walk to a paralysed man, and so on. There could be no question of the power of Jesus to change even congenital conditions and so transform the life of a disabled person. But he didn't heal all the disabled people he met on his travels. The beggar who was healed when Peter and John went into the Temple (Acts 3:1-10) was almost certainly there on the occasions when Jesus had earlier visited the Temple. Jesus was very selective when he healed one man by the Pool of Siloam even though 'a great many disabled people' were there. (John 5:1-9)

The fact that some disabled people are not healed is not to deny the possibility of healing. Clearly God is able to restore a disabled person to a fully functioning, able-bodied individual and from time to time has done so. What is in question is whether that is invariably his purpose; experience and Scripture suggest that it is not. That being so the church must be prepared to respond to people as they are, with or without disabilities, and where necessary take steps to ensure that they are able to enter fully into the life of the fellowship.

DISABILITY AND HOPE

Theology has a good deal to say about what happens when Jesus comes again - an issue of considerable difference of view - what happens when we die, and what heaven is like, but it has little to say about the place of disability in all of this. Just about the only thing we can say with certainty is that we are not certain as to what the Bible means when it speaks of 'the last things'. The writers seem to struggle to express in terms that we can understand the wonders and glories of eternity of which they were given a glimpse. It is clearly wonderful beyond words.

The general assumption we make is that the entrance to heaven will be littered with discarded crutches, wheelchairs, spectacles and disability aids of all sorts. Certainly there will be no need for them in heaven.

Joni Eareckson-Tada, someone who became quadriplegic as the result of a diving accident, anticipates being able to dance and run and jump again. But does that mean that all evidence of previous disabilities will be gone?

Paul explains that following the resurrection we will be given a new body, a spiritual body. (It is worth reading 1 Cor 15:35-49 to get the full picture.) This will be different from the earthly body but related to it in the way that a plant is related to the seed from which it grew. Quite what that will mean in practice we are not told and could probably not understand anyway. But how will a person be affected who has a life defining disability, like Down's syndrome?

Prof John Swinton tells of a mortuary caretaker speaking about a Ian, a man with Down's syndrome who had died.

> 'He'll not have Down's syndrome because he'll have a resurrection body.' Now, he is 'like us'. In other words the resurrection body is perceived to be the body of an able-bodied person no longer burdened by genetic difference. But why would this be considered a good thing? What exactly does God think is wrong with Down's syndrome that it is not to be represented in the resurrection body? What does it say about the value of Ian's body now, in the present, if [he is] to be transformed or perhaps even 'healed' in the eschaton? What exactly would be healed? Who would Ian be in his new and alien body?[1]

And while you are wondering about the implications of this, remember that Jesus still had scars in his resurrection body! Of course there will be no disabilities in heaven, but will all those characteristics that are an essential aspect of who we are and the lives we have lived simply cease to be? We don't have answers to such questions, but we should, perhaps, reflect on what they might say to our attitudes to people with disabilities here and now.

Notes

[1] Swinton, John, Mowat, Harriet and Baines, Susannah (2011) *Whose Story Am I? Redescribing Profound Intellectual Disability in the Kingdom of God,* Journal of Religion, Disability and Health, 15:1,8

See also Tony Phelps-Jones, *Making Church Accessible to All,* obtainable from Prospects at www.prospects.org.uk

APPENDIX E
THE PROSPECTS STORY AND VISION

If ever the full story of life for people with learning disabilities is told it will show that, with few exceptions, for century after century they were excluded from and ignored by mainstream society in Britain - and, perhaps, elsewhere. In the past 150 years that exclusion took the form of long-stay institutions. Large numbers of people were 'warehoused' in isolated 'hospitals for the mentally subnormal' to which they were sent in infancy or adolescence and where they would usually remain until they died. Many, of course, lived with their parents but always with the dread that if the time came when the family could not cope the institution was the likely solution. People with learning disabilities were even excluded from otherwise universal services like education. Although the medieval mumblings about demonisation had more or less ceased by the 20th century, the stigma of learning disability hung like a dark cloud over people with learning disabilities and their families.

Things began to change in the 1970s, a decade which was to prove a turning point in the story. Looking back only four decades later it is hard to believe that attitudes and services have changed so much in so short a time. One of the first indicators of change was the publication of a government command document in 1971: Better Services for the Mentally Handicapped. A year later the Department of Education took responsibility for the education of children with special needs. At first this amounted to little more than a re-labelling of the existing service provided by NHS staff largely untrained for this specialised task. Several new charitable organizations trace their origins from this period.

Having a child with Down's syndrome, Madeleine and I were drawn into the sub-culture of families similar to our own. We observed that many of the parents we met were elderly but still bearing the full care of an adult son or daughter with a learning disability. The concern expressed time and time again by such people was for the future of their son or daughter when they could no longer provide the care and support needed. As Rachel was our first child, and we were still young, it was not an issue for us, but as a pastor I wondered what Christian parents did in the event of breakdown or crisis. We decided to find out what Christian provision existed for adults with learning disabilities. It was a shock to find that it was almost non-existent. This discovery led to the writing of an article under the headline, A Cause for Concern. It appeared in the November 1973 issue of the *Evangelical Times.*

The article received such a strong response from families around the country that it was clear that something had to be done; hence the founding in 1976 of a charity which took the headline as its working title, now known as Prospects. By the end of the 1970s the first home had been opened in Aberystwyth in partnership with Alfred Place Baptist Church. Property was also being refurbished in Reading with the support of Carey Baptist Church. It began to take in residents in 1982, by which time properties were being prepared in Maidstone, Bournemouth and Deganwy.

Learning disability came to public attention during the 1980s, in part because of a shocking documentary of life in the 'mental subnormality hospitals'. 'A Silent Witness' reported abuse and mistreatment on a huge scale. It created a sense of urgency for change. Different approaches to the care and support of people with learning disabilities were pioneered. New ways of thinking emerged within the profession with the intention of 'normalising' life for people with learning disabilities. State funding for care went through major changes - at first generous, then followed by u-turns because of the larger than expected costs encountered. Prospects was a participant in these changes and was challenged to think Biblically about its attitudes and to find ways of applying Biblical principles to its thinking and practices. It was during this period that the Principle of Personal Value was developed. (See Chapter 2)

Ten years on from its founding, Prospects had operational homes in Aberystwyth, Reading, Bournemouth, Maidstone and Deganwy. A second property was bought in Reading and another was to be built in the grounds of the home in Aberystwyth. Plans were in hand to develop in Bayston Hill near Shrewsbury, in each case at the invitation of local churches. Growing interest was also evident in Northern Ireland.

There was another significant development taking place within the organisation. In 1983 Madeleine had been concerned that residents of Helena House, the Prospects home in Reading, should have the opportunity to understand the Gospel more fully. Sunday services were not sufficiently accessible to them because of their limitations. So she began a Bible group with the aim of helping them grasp what God is like. From the very first meeting it was evident that this was an unmet need. Unable to find any resources appropriate to the limitations of people with learning disabilities, she developed her own. Before long these were being requested by others. In due course Prospects encouraged the growth of church based local groups. Invitations to provide ministry for people with learning disabilities attending major Christian conventions and holiday conferences led to more people becoming aware of the opportunities to reach out to people with learning disabilities in their own communities. So far as we can discover, no similar attempt has been made in church history, to reach people with learning disabilities with the Gospel!

This coincided with an increased rate of closure of long-stay institutions. More and more people with learning disabilities began to live in small groups in the community, and more and more were to be found attending church services. This further encouraged churches to take positive steps to respond to them in ways that would be meaningful for them.

By the time of its 25th anniversary in 2001, Prospects had become a significant force in the field of learning disability. It had gained in size and status to the point that it would be able to sustain considerable growth in the next decade. The figures speak for themselves, especially when updated to include the current position:

	1976	2001	2013
No. of people served by Prospects services	0	125	325
No. of people served by Prospects ministry groups	0	1500	3000
No. of Prospects ministry groups	0	122	210
No. of staff employed	1	250	770
Annual turnover	£2.4k	£3.9m	£12m

As well as its work in the UK Prospects has partnered and supported Christian agencies in other countries. Currently it is involved with projects in Romania and India. It is also involved with a network of Christian disability organisations across Europe.

However, encouraging as it is to see the way Prospects has grown over the years there is still a great deal of unmet need. It is estimated that the number of adults with learning disabilities in Christian families living with carers over 70 years of age runs to 3,000-4,000.* For each of these families the need for long-term support could become critical at any time. Which is why Prospects still has a vision for ongoing development to provide a Christian service for as many as seek it by working with groups of families in locations where there is a need.

The greatest challenge over the years has been to maintain the Christian ethos of Prospects. At the outset Madeleine and I saw the Charity as an expression of God's heart for people with learning disabilities. We determined that Biblical principles would be applied to every aspect of Prospects activities. That has not always been possible to achieve but the effort continues. There have been disappointments as some of the homes had to close for varied reasons. We take encouragement from the fact that when Madeleine and I had to step down from leadership because of health problems, others equally committed to their Christian faith and to people with learning disabilities have been available to build Prospects into the Christian and professional organisation it has become.

Prospects is a Christian organisation which values and support people with learning disabilities so that they live their lives to the full.

For more information about the services and ministry of Prospects see www. prospects.org.uk or write to Prospects, 69 Honey End Lane, Reading RG30 4EL.

---

*This figure is an estimate of the proportion of Christians among the 29,000 people in the UK living with carers over 70 years of age.

APPENDIX F
THE CARE STORY AND VISION

It has been said that the 1960s shaped the Britain of today. It is certainly true that some of the liberal legislation passed around that time, and some of the cultural changes in the UK, did have a huge impact on what is now accepted in society.

Some have asked 'Where was the Church when all this happened? After all, Christians are called to be salt and light, to influence society for good.' I would tell them how, in 1971, an unprecedented movement of Christians of many denominations rallied together - from every part of the UK. On Friday evening, 24 September of that year, beacons were lit across the country. The following day tens of thousands of people descended on London's Trafalgar Square and in other city centres to stand up for truth and righteousness. It was described as a 'Nationwide Festival of Light'. This resulted in a the setting up of a charity of the same name, voicing a genuine concern about the effects on society of rapid legislative change on a range of social and moral issues. There was a need to develop a structured response that could challenge and influence government policy, a Christian voice into Parliament. So a small basement office was set up in the vicarage of Christ Church Mayfair. Raymond Johnston was the first Director with Charlie Colchester and Lyndon Bowring - who was appointed Executive Chairman in 1981.

Out of this organisation, CARE was launched two years later at an evening event in the Barbican, in the City of London, with John Stott giving the keynote address - which incidentally is the final chapter in his seminal work Issues Facing Christians Today. CARE began to produce research and write briefings and speeches for MPs and Peers. Biblical truth was being declared but, alongside this, emerged a desire to also demonstrate Christ's compassion. For example, if we were campaigning against abortion, there was also the need to help women facing an unplanned pregnancy. With the assistance of Dr Anne Townsend, CARE began to support Christians as they showed God's love in action. The most notable results were the CARE's Homes Programme, with hundreds of Christians opening their homes to people under pressure for short breaks and sometimes longer stays and, subsequently, fostering projects for children in need. Stories began to emerge of lives turned around through Christian hospitality.

A huge opportunity emerged when a group called 'Christians Caring for Life' asked to come under CARE's umbrella. What is now known as CareConfidential was born. There are now scores of centres all over the UK providing support for women facing an unexpected pregnancy or post abortion trauma. Through God's grace thousands of lives were touched and many unborn children saved.

Wherever possible, CARE has sought to link together two sides of the same coin: research and advocacy with caring for the most vulnerable people in our society. From the very beginning human dignity, stemming from the truth that we are all made in the image of God, is the golden thread which has run through the work of CARE. Our focus has always been to promote policies that protect the unborn, the newly born child with special needs, those with learning disabilities, frail elderly people and more recently those who have been trafficked for commercial sexual exploitation. The vision has also been for a society where marriage and a loving family life are honoured. This is why CARE began a department called Care for the Family - which, now a self-standing organisation, is one of Britain's best-known Christian charities.

CARE was involved in education, pioneering training for School Governors, encouraging prayer for schools, and **evaluate…informing choice**, a relationships and sex education programme which seeks to empower young people to make healthy decisions about their relationships.

But perhaps the greatest long-term influence in our national life is CARE's Leadership Programme, investing young people with the potential to be the leaders of the future. Taking young graduates for a year, we equip them with a biblical worldview to go out into public life. To date among the alumni of the Leadership Programme - over 200 of them - are MPs and others working in Parliament, members of the Diplomatic Service, the Civil Service, local government and the media, Christians seeding society with God's grace and truth.

Some of the challenges we face in the twenty-first century are very different from those of the 1960s - although some stay the same. Internet safety, particularly for children, is one example. As society changes at an ever increasing pace, the issues we research and campaign about will continue to develop so as to be relevant to the needs of the day. We must continue to 'understand the times' and seize the opportunities God gives us to speak out and serve others.

Nola Leach, Chief Executive, CARE

ACKNOWLEDGEMENTS

Anybody who has ever attempted to write a book knows that they stand on the shoulders of other people. Without doubt they are very many in my case. But I want to acknowledge some who have had a more than passing influence in my thinking, in my ability as a writer and in my development as a person. Peter Masters and I worked alongside one another as editors of Evangelical Times in the 1970s. His belief in my ability and his guidance made me a better writer. Bob Horn then took over from Peter and his wisdom and friendship aided a stronger grasp of Biblical theology. Peter Levell became a member of the board of Prospects only a year or two after its commencement then, many years later, took the role of Chief Executive. His friendship and personal support has meant more than I can express. And his ability as an editor has greatly improved what you hold in your hands. Peter Oakes worked with me in Prospects for only five years but it was a period of immense importance in developing my understanding of people with learning disabilities. I am grateful to the Principal and Librarian of Wales Evangelical School of Theology (WEST) for help in sourcing material during the study for this book.

Another person from whom I learned so many lessons was Rachel, our daughter with Down's syndrome. She became a gracious Christian lady with a remarkable capacity for love. Her sensitivity, courtesy, generosity and kindness will never be forgotten. Hundreds gathered from all over the country to celebrate her life following her death in August 2012 at the age of 49.

Most writers also acknowledge the support of their wife as they have been writing. I want to do the same and say a huge thank you to Madeleine. Only those who have walked this path will know how understanding and patient one's wife has to be. She must listen patiently as we try to resolve how to express what we want to say.

She must bear those moments during dinner when we drift off with some new idea for making our point on paper. She accepts without complaint the nights when we are restless because our brain insists on pursuing a better turn of phrase. Madeleine has been the single most important human being in my life and has given me more than she can ever know.

COMMENDATIONS

'No-one knows more about caring and thinking like a Christian in modern Britain than David Potter, and Christians will find this book a sure-footed guide to help them walk alongside him.'

NIGEL CAMERON, WRITER AND SPEAKER

'There are many things that I appreciate about David Potter. Perhaps the greatest is a remarkable presence of God I sense when he prays. The other is the legacy of Prospects which offers fullness of life for people with learning disability.'

MATT BIRD, CHAIR, THE CINNAMON NETWORK

'With the continual rise of secularism and humanism in our current age, David Potter reminds us of the basic yet powerful principles of God's continuing justice and righteous ways, which are firmly rooted in His love for mankind. This book helps give us timely insight as to how to deal with many current and controversial issues and how to stand against them lovingly and in God's truth.'

AMANDA DYE

'David Potter has written a masterly, easy-to-read exposition about the nature of Christian love in action, countering secularism and the new atheism with a clear biblical response. After reading it you will find yourself drawn to those for whom the need to be valued is the greatest. It is a superb exposition of what it means to be made in the image of God, and how we should apply this precious truth.'

LYNDON BOWRING